Happy Reading Fort

Brian

Royal Children

For Vanessa

Royal Children

NICHOLAS COURTNEY

Fitzhenry & Whiteside

First published 1982
© Nicholas Courtney 1982

Fitzhenry & Whiteside Limited
150 Lesmill Road,
Don Mills, Ontario M3B 2T5

ISBN 0-88902-719-6

Acknowledgments

The author and publishers would like to thank the following for their kind permission to reproduce the photographs in this book:

Colour photographs

Reproduced by gracious permission of Her Majesty the Queen: 8; Associated Newspapers: 7; BBC Hulton Picture Library: 2, 11, 12, 13; Camera Press Ltd: 1, 14, 17, 24 (Photo: Snowdon); Central Press Photos Ltd: 16; Fox Photos Ltd: 3, 4, 15, 18, 19, 20, 21, 22; Peter A. Harding: 23; Press Association Ltd: 5, 6; John Topham Picture Library: 9, 10

Black and white photographs

Reproduced by gracious permission of Her Majesty the Queen: 23, 24, 25, 26, 28, 31, 32, 33, 34, 35, 37, 38, 52; BBC Hulton Picture Library: 9, 29, 30, 39, 44, 50, 59, 63, 64; Camera Press Ltd: 43, 51, 68, 71, 73, 92a, 92b; Central Press Photos Ltd: 70, 75, 81, 82, 83; Crown Copyright (DoE): 93; Crown Copyright (Victoria & Albert Museum): 4; Eastern Daily Press: 18, 21; Fox Photos Ltd: 12, 13, 53, 54, 55, 60, 72, 74, 78, 86; James Hancock: 16, 17; Peter A. Harding: 5, 94; Imperial War Museum: 62; Popperfoto Ltd: 27, 40, 41, 46, 56, 66; Press Association Ltd: 19, 20; Sir Geoffrey Shakerley: 22; Syndication International: 36, 42, 47, 88, 90, 91, 92c; The Times: 45; John Topham Picture Library: 6, 7, 8, 10, 11, 14, 15, 48, 49, 57, 58, 61, 65, 67, 69, 76, 77, 79, 80, 84, 85, 87, 89; Victoria & Albert Museum: 4

CONTENTS

In the preparation of this book, I have drawn on the writings, remembrances and help of many people. I would like to acknowledge their assistance collectively but in particular the Press Office of Buckingham Palace and the members of the families and friends of both the Prince and Princess of Wales. Also, I would like to thank HRH The Duchess of Gloucester for permission to use her account of the birth of the late Prince William of Gloucester and Miss Elizabeth Ridesdale, former headmistress of Riddlesworth School, for permission to reproduce her account of the Princess of Wales's time at her school.

For the illustrations, I am most grateful to HM The Queen for her gracious permission to reproduce her photographs from the Royal Archives, Windsor and a painting from Buckingham Palace. I would also like to thank the staff of the Royal Archives, Windsor Castle for their help, in particular Miss Frances Dimond, curator of the Photographic Department; and also Jim Hancock, for the use of his private photographs.

Finally, I would like to thank the Hon. Ursula Wyndham for compiling the index.

INTRODUCTION

The Royal Baby

The role of every monarchy is to serve (Ich Dein) its subjects. The goal of every royal house is continuity and, with the birth of H.R.H. The Prince William Arthur Philip Louis, son and heir to the Prince and Princess of Wales, those aims of the Royal Family are now firmly re-established, and their line secure into the second half of the twenty-first century. The infant Prince, second in line in succession to the throne, will be the forty-second monarch since his namesake, William the Conqueror.

At five a.m. on Monday, 21 June 1982, the Princess of Wales, accompanied by her husband, left for St Mary's, a teaching hospital in Paddington. The Princess was admitted to the Lindo Wing where her room was unremarkable save for its plainness. News of her arrival precipitated a steady stream of well-wishers who joined the tight knot of press photographers and television cameras outside the main entrance to the Lindo Wing and there they remained, despite the heavy rain, for the rest of the day.

When the Princess arrived at the hospital, she was in the early stages of labour. The Prince of Wales, as he had often indicated before, stayed with his wife throughout the whole of her sixteen-hour labour and was thrilled to be present at the actual birth of their son at 9.03 that evening. It was very nearly a natural birth. In an interview later, George Pinker confirmed 'Yes it was . . . well almost. Just at the end the Princess did have a bit of pain relief, but I'm afraid I can't go into details.'

The Prince of Wales admitted later that night that being a father was 'rather a grown-up thing. Rather a shock to my system.'

William, as Buckingham Place was to announce his name a week later, weighed 7 lb $1\frac{1}{2}$ oz at birth, like all royal babies 'cried lustily' and had a wisp of fair hair, 'sort of blondish' and blue eyes.

The smaller crowd waiting outside Buckingham Palace witnessed the official bulletin being placed on a brass easel behind the gates which confirmed that 'Her Royal Highness and her child are both doing well.' Within the Palace, the Queen and Prince Philip, together with the whole Household, celebrated the birth with champagne, while below, in the Palace Post Office, telegrams were sent to all

Commonwealth leaders, Heads of State and Ambassadors throughout the world. In the House of Commons, a cheer went up as Speaker Thomas announced the birth. The Archbishop of Canterbury, Dr Robert Runcie, echoed the thoughts of the nation when he said 'We rejoice with them. It is good news for millions around the World who hold them in their affection and their prayers.'

The Archbishop was right and the news of the birth was the lead story in every continent the next day. The Princess of Wales, who had endeared herself to the whole world from the start of her courtship, now added yet another chapter to the fairy tale of her life when she gave birth to her first child, a son and an heir.

Further news of the mother and baby came when members of both families visited the Princess of Wales in hospital. The Hon. Mrs Peter Shand Kydd reported 'She [the Princess of Wales] is looking radiant, absolutely radiant. My grandson is a lovely baby. There is a great deal of happiness in there.' Earl Spencer, the Princess's father, declared that 'He [William] is the most beautiful baby I have ever seen,' while Prince Charles commented that his son 'was looking a little bit more human this morning'.

At one o'clock precisely, at the express wish of the Queen, two forty-one gun salutes were fired simultaneously by the King's Troop, Royal Horse Artillery in Hyde Park and the Honourable Artillery Company at the Tower of London. Meanwhile, throughout London and Great Britain, church bells were rung in celebration of the birth.

Shortly after six o'clock that evening, the Princess of Wales left hospital, thirty-six hours after her arrival. By leaving so soon after the birth of William, just twenty-one hours, she again displayed her own independent character and modern approach to motherhood. Her gynaecologist confirmed that her decision 'would not cause any problems' as mother and child would fare better at Kensington Palace with the monthly nurse, Sister Anne Wallace, to care for them both. A loud cheer went up as the Prince and Princess of Wales appeared at the door of the Lindo Wing, he holding the day-old William. At the bottom of the steps, Prince Charles handed the baby to his wife and paused only briefly before ushering mother and son into the car to be driven home to Kensington Palace.

The announcement that the Princess was expecting her first baby was made by Buckingham Palace on the morning of 5 November, barely a hundred days after the Royal Wedding. The bulletin continued:

> The Prince and Princess of Wales, the Queen and the Duke of Edinburgh and members of both families are delighted by the news. The Queen was informed personally by the Prince and Princess.
>
> The Princess is in excellent health. Her doctor during the pregnancy will be Mr George Pinker, Surgeon-Gynaecologist to the Queen.
>
> The Princess hopes to continue to undertake some public engagements but regrets any disappointment which may be caused by any curtailment to her planned programme.
>
> The baby will be second in line to the throne.

BUCKINGHAM PALACE

Her Royal Highness The Princess of Wales
was safely delivered of a son at 9.03 P.M. today.

Her Royal Highness and her child are both
doing well.

Signed ....

....

....

....

21st June 1982.

1. The official announcement of the birth of Prince William of Wales posted behind the gates of Buckingham Palace on 21 June 1982. The bulletin is signed by Mr John Batten, head of the Queen's medical household. Mr Clive Roberts, the anaesthetist, Mr David Harvey, the Princess of Wales's paediatrician, and finally Mr George Pinker, the Surgeon-Gynaecologist to the Queen.

The style and timing of the Palace announcement were a departure from their usual form. For example, when the Queen was expecting Prince Charles, the public were left to draw their own conclusions from a curt piece in the Court Circular which read: 'Her Royal Highness, Duchess of Edinburgh, will undertake no public engagements after the end of June.' The Princess of Wales's news was broken earlier than usual so that her proposed tour with Prince Charles

2. The first view of Prince William in the arms of the Prince of Wales at the door of the Lindo Wing, St Mary's Hospital, Paddington, the day after he was born, 22 June 1982. It was the Princess of Wales's own decision to return to Kensington Palace just twenty-one hours after the birth.

3. The Prince of Wales, who was present at the birth, carefully hands Prince William to his mother as they prepare to leave the hospital.

of Australia and New Zealand could be cancelled before the preparations were too advanced.

Even without the announcement, there were several clues that the Princess was pregnant, like the flying visit she made to London from Balmoral on 14 October to see her gynaecologist, George Pinker. Then on 30 November, the last day of the highly successful, but gruelling tour of Wales, both Prince Charles and the Princess visited the same maternity ward of Llwynypia Hospital. According to a young mother with a new-born baby, the Princess cried: '"Oh, babies", before rushing over to see our children. She asked lots of questions about labour and peeped into the cot to see my baby boy.' Another new mother remarked that 'even Prince Charles was quizzing the mothers about how long they had been in labour, and the Princess asked me how I managed to keep my baby so quiet.' Prince Charles told another that he thought it was 'a very good thing for a husband to be with the mother when she was having her baby', adding to the attendant pressmen, 'I expect I'll get lots of letters about that.' The tour of Wales was a resounding success for the Princess, especially considering she was suffering from morning sickness throughout. The final clue that the Princess of Wales was pregnant came in London when she did not go on to dine with the Italian Ambassador after the reception to mark the opening of the *Splendours of the Gonzaga* at the Victoria and Albert Museum. It was reported that she was 'unwell'.

The next day, after the Buckingham Palace statement, the Prince and Princess of Wales went to the Guildhall for a City of London lunch given by the Lord Mayor, Sir Ronald Gardner, In a hastily rewritten, flowery speech he eulogized : 'The magic of the Royal Wedding has provided a memory that glows with the everlasting lustre of a gold ingot. A gold ingot that has now been supremely hallmarked by this morning's announcement that Your Royal Highnesses are to be blessed with a child, which we all rejoice 'remembering that babies are bits of stardust blown from the hand of God.' His speech, like the news of the pregnancy throughout the United Kingdom, was greeted with rapturous applause.

While the nation, still heady from the splendours of the Royal Wedding, rejoiced at the news of the pregnancy, the bookmakers were offering odds of anything between 50 and 125 to 1 on the possibility of twins—generous odds considering that the Prince and Princess of Wales have several sets of twins in their families. The Princess's paternal aunt, Lady Anne Hughes-Wake-Walker, has a twin boy and girl, her maternal aunt, Mary, has twin daughters, her grandfather, Lord Fermoy, had an identical twin brother, Francis, and Ruth, Lady Fermoy is the daughter of a twin. Twins in the Royal Family are less common. In the twentieth century the only twins were born to two of the Queen Mother's brothers, one of whom had a twin boy and girl and the other twin girls.

In the early months of the Princess of Wales's pregnancy, she suffered badly from morning sickness. She managed to attend the Service of Remembrance at the Cenotaph on Sunday 8 November but cancelled her engagement in the afternoon. She called off her visit to the Duchy of Cornwall for the same reason. The Prince of Wales, with characteristic concern for his wife, explained her absence by saying, 'You have all got wives—you know the problems. She is all right, but it is better not to do too many things.' Buckingham Palace added : 'The Princess has made it known that she will try to make as many public appearances as possible, but if she does not feel well she will have to withdraw. In her condition she is bound to have some days off.' In fact, she only cancelled one other engagement, a visit to Bristol with Prince Charles on 17 November.

Time and again, however, the Princess of Wales showed that her pregnancy did not interfere with the heavy schedule of engagements. On 4 November, she attended the State Opening of Parliament, a dazzling affair where she was the centre of attraction. A week later, she accompanied Prince Charles to Derbyshire and to the Railway Museum in York. Although feeling distinctly unwell, she went on to open a shopping centre in Chesterfield. She confided with one mother there that, 'some days I feel terrible. No one told me I would feel like I did'. Some of her official engagements gave her considerable personal pleasure, like the planting of a tulip tree with Prince Charles for their baby, then a mountain ash to commemorate

4. The Prince and Princess of Wales with the wife of the Italian Ambassador, Signora Cagiagi, at the opening of the *Splendours of the Gonzaga* exhibition at the Victoria and Albert Museum on 4 November 1981—the day before the announcement of the Princess's pregnancy.

their wedding. The next day, 20 November, she managed to lunch with her father, Earl Spencer, and her stepmother at her old home, Althorp, before driving to Northampton to open the new Post Office.

However taxing these engagements were, there were, in between, extensive periods of holiday and plenty of time for the Princess of Wales to rest and live the normal life of a young married woman expecting her first baby. After the wedding and honeymoon, there was a long run-in to her rounds of official duties. She and Prince Charles spent nearly ten weeks at Balmoral, half of it at Craigowan, a small house on the estate. There they led a simple life, free from all outside pressures and indeed away from other members of the Royal Family. As they walked the hills or fished the River Dee, they were on their own for practically the first time since their courtship began. On Christmas Eve, they joined the Royal Family at Windsor, then moved on to Sandringham shortly before the New Year. For the Princess of Wales it was like going home, for she had been born and had spent her childhood in a house on the estate. She was able to visit her Norfolk friends and the places she loved as a girl. Later, Buckingham Palace disclosed that she had fallen down the stairs at Sandringham, but added, 'a local doctor was called in, and subsequently the Princess's own gynaecologist, and there is no cause for concern. She is perfectly fit and well.' The announcement was supported by Mr Pinker who confirmed there was 'no hint of any trouble. She is a strong and healthy young woman.'

Outside her official functions, the Princess of Wales lived as free and normal a life as the press and public would allow. During her Scottish holiday in the autumn, she flew twice to London to visit the exhibition of her wedding presents at St James's Palace and made the final arrangements to move some of them down to Highgrove, the house that Prince Charles had bought the year before near Tetbury in Gloucestershire. Up to 17 May 1982, when the Prince and Princess of Wales moved into their apartments at Kensington Palace, Highgrove was their only home. They are now both very much part of the Gloucestershire community and take great interest in their local town. In return, the local people are protective towards their new neighbours. They were thrilled when the Prince and Princess of Wales attended the 'Evening of Christmas Music' at St Mary's Church on 6 December and, two days later, braving the snow, when the Princess visited the local school.

During her pregnancy, the Princess occasionally managed to slip back unobserved to the Young England Kindergarten in Pimlico, in London, the school where she taught before her marriage. Prince Charles was even persuaded to play Father Christmas at their Christmas party. But now as a married woman and the Princess of Wales, she naturally began to see less of her own friends. She did not, however, lose all contact. An avid letter-writer, she keeps in touch with them signing herself with, and being addressed by her nickname, 'Duchess'. She spent much of her time shopping for clothes for herself and buying everything for her baby, but the attentions of the press and insatiable curiosity of the British public spoilt what is one of her principal pleasures.

The dogging of the Princess's every move was not confined to London. A constant corps of camera-men had Highgrove virtually under siege. The house is vulnerable since it is close to the road, within sight of a public Right of Way. The grass at every vantage point has been worn bare by photographers. Today, the boundary ditch has been dug out and the spoil acts as an earth rampart, affording, with the newly-planted trees, a little more privacy.

The press were in position during the first weekend of December when the Prince and Princess of Wales gave their first house-party. From their vantage points, they photographed them dancing outside their front door, watched by their guests—among them, her sister, Lady Sarah McCorquodale, and her husband Neil, Lady Sarah Armstrong-Jones, Prince Charles's old friend Nicholas Soames and his wife Caroline, and Lord Patrick Beresford. The Princess had been photographed every time she went to Tetbury to shop or walked in the garden, but the house-party photographs were too much of an intrusion to ignore. The Fleet Street editors were invited to Buckingham Palace and asked by the Queen

5. By now very much part of the Gloucestershire community, the Princess of Wales talks to Dominic White, the soloist, at a concert of Christmas Music at Tetbury Parish Church on 6 December 1981.

personally to call off their reporters and only cover the Princess's official visits. It was a heartfelt appeal from a mother for her pregnant daughter-in-law.

The press embargo on candid, unofficial photographs of the Princess of Wales was immediately honoured, but two months later it was broken by the *Sun* and *Daily Star*. Their reporters and photographers followed her and Prince Charles, with their hosts Lord and Lady Romsey, to the West Indian island of Eleuthera. The photographs of the Princess, five months pregnant, wearing only a bikini on the beach, that appeared in those newspapers caused a storm of indignation. The Queen was furious and her Press Secretary, Michael Shea, condemned outright the pictures and the article: 'Such tasteless behaviour is in breach of normally accepted British Press standards in respect of the privacy of individuals.' Despite this upset, the Princess returned to London on 26 February looking fit, healthy and thoroughly rested.

All through her pregnancy, the Princess of Wales demonstrated that she is a thoroughly modern mother. She kept up her official engagements, ending with a visit to Liverpool on 2 April, then opening the new Sony factory at Brigend in Glamorgan five days later and finally, on 18 May, just five weeks before her baby was born, she stood in for the Queen Mother when she opened 'The Albany' in Deptford, the new headquarters for one of her patronages, Children at Risk. Her private life was full and active as well. She went with her amateur jockey husband to the Cheltenham National Hunt Festival and, judging by the press photographs, she did not enjoy that cold day of racing as much as the Grand National at Aintree which they attended on 4 April. On Easter Sunday, they took Holy Communion together at the Parish Church of St Mary's in Tetbury, giving the vicar, Michael Sherwood, only five minutes warning. For their final holiday before the birth of their baby, Prince Charles took his wife to his cottage, Tamarisk, on Tresco—one of the Scilly Isles.

During her first year of marriage and her pregnancy, the Princess of Wales has proved, by her popularity, energy and sense of duty, that she is well suited for the role as wife of the Heir Apparent. In that time, she has gained a marked maturity, not only in her appearance but in outlook as well. Now, as mother of William, second in line to the throne, the Princess of Wales has established a role in her own right and achieved a true identity for herself.

PART ONE

The Royal Parents

1

Charles

On the evening of 14 November 1948, Sir Alan Lascelles, King George VI's private secretary, hurried down the long corridors of Buckingham Palace to the squash court behind the swimming pool. There he found Prince Philip playing squash with his private secretary and friend, Lieutenant-Commander Michael Parker. Sir Alan burst onto the court and announced that Princess Elizabeth had given birth to a son.

Prince Philip, dressed in a pair of white flannel trousers and shirt, threw down his racket and ran to the Buhl Room which had been converted into a makeshift surgery, where his wife, Princess Elizabeth, was still drowsy after the effects of the anaesthetic. Next door he was congratulated by his parents-in-law, King George VI and Queen Elizabeth, spoke briefly to the team of gynaecologists and doctors, headed by Sir William Gilliat and the King's physician, Sir John Weir. Prince Philip then went to see his son in the care of the royal midwife, Miss Helen Rowe, in the nursery. When Elizabeth had recovered from the anaesthetic, Prince Philip presented her with a large bunch of red carnations and roses.

Outside Buckingham Palace, a large crowd of people, many thousands strong, had braved the damp and chilly weather since the early hours of the morning, each no doubt hoping to be the first to hear the news of the birth. They were rewarded when a blue-liveried footman crossed the Palace courtyard and whispered into the ear of one of the many policemen who vainly tried to protect the guardsmen on duty outside the railings. The policeman yelled, 'It's a boy' and the message spread like wildfire through the crowd. They began to sing, 'For he's a jolly good fellow' and chant 'We want Philip'. The King's Press Secretary, Commander Richard Colville, wrote in his own neat hand the announcement that was put up on the Palace railings—'Her Royal Highness the Princess Elizabeth, Duchess of Edinburgh, was safely delivered of a Prince at 9.14 o'clock this evening. Her Royal Highness and the infant Prince are both doing well.'

The news of the birth was quickly dispatched around the world, to all crowned heads and presidents, heads of Commonwealth, Governors and ambassadors, by telegram, with the word 'Prince' added to the prepared text. It was also relayed over the wireless and soon beacons were blazing all over the

6. A jubilant crowd outside the gates of Buckingham Palace celebrating the news of the birth of Prince Charles on 14 November 1948.

country. In London the fountains in Trafalgar Square were turned blue, for a boy, and remained that colour for a week.

The roar and cheers of the crowd were heard in Marlborough House by Queen Mary, who had already been informed by telephone of the birth. The venerable octogenarian Queen was driven the short distance to Buckingham Palace to see her first great-grandson at eleven o'clock and stayed, despite her recent attack of influenza, until after midnight.

Meanwhile the shouts of the people outside and the blasts on their car horns could be heard in the first-floor rooms overlooking the Mall where the Princess was naturally elated but tired after the birth. Sleep was impossible and she asked if something could be done to quieten the crowd. Commander Parker and a colleague walked over to the railings and tackled the nearest person to ask for quiet, hoping the message could be spread as fast as the news of the birth. That person happened to be David Niven, the well-known English actor. He was 'pinned against the railings and, being unable to move, was the recipient of the message hissed in my ear by the man from the Palace . . . I turned round and tried

19

to shush those nearest to me, which did little good as everyone was far too excited and happy.' Finally the police were called and the crowd were dispersed with appeals from loudspeakers.

There was one break with tradition for this royal birth. The King had decreed that the Home Secretary should not be present in the Palace as witness, the procedure being an archaic custom 'for which there was no legal requirement'. The custom has been dropped for every subsequent royal birth and, in 1982, there was no question of reviving it for the present Prince and Princess of Wales's baby.

A week before the birth, Sir Alan Lascelles had pointed out to the King that, as the constitution stood, the children of the sovereign's daughter would not have the title of Prince or Princess. The King had already conferred on Prince Philip the style of Royal Highness and the titles of Duke of Edinburgh, Earl of Merioneth and Baron Greenwich, as well as raising him to the Order of the Garter. As Prince Philip had relinquished his Greek and Danish titles when he married, he reverted to his mother's name of Battenburg, which had been anglicised to Mountbatten. Thus his children would have been simply Charles Mountbatten, Earl of Merioneth or the Lady Anne Mountbatten. By Letters Patent under the Great Seal, the King now ordered that all children born to the Duke and Duchess of Edinburgh should bear the style of Royal Highness with the title of Prince and Princess.

The day after the birth, the celebrations began in earnest. Gun salutes from ships and shore batteries resounded throughout the country, while church bells pealed incessantly. It was not only Great Britain who celebrated the birth in high style. Every Commonwealth capital was also bedecked with bunting and flags. On a more artistic level the Poet Laureate, John Masefield, wrote a four-line poem, *A Hope for the Newly Born* —

> May destiny, allotting what befalls,
> Grant to the newly born this saving grace,
> And guard more sure than ships and fortress-walls,
> The loyal love and service of a race.

— while the BBC commissioned three British composers, Michael Tippett, Gordon Jacob and Herbert Howells, to write a piece called 'Music for a Prince' in honour of the birth.

Letters, telegrams and presents poured in from all over the world. Conscious of the wartime shortages, the United States' gift was a ton-and-a-half of nappies which were distributed to needy mothers throughout England. The only alarm in the general rejoicing were reports that there might be something wrong with the baby, but the record was quickly put straight with a speech from the Queen's sister, Countess Granville, to the Girl Guides in Northern Ireland: '. . . he could not be more angelic-looking. He is golden-haired and has the most beautiful complexion, as well as amazingly delicate features for so young a baby . . .'

Prince Philip and Princess Elizabeth were especially proud of their baby and the Princess wrote to a friend, 'It's wonderful to think, isn't it, that his arrival could give a bit of happiness to so many people, besides ourselves, at this time?' She thought he had his father's smile while Prince Philip, according to his childhood friend Hélène Cordet, thought that he looked like a plum pudding. Cecil Beaton, who took the first photographs of the Prince, was struck by his 'remarkably long and pointed fingers' but thought he had the look of Queen Mary. Queen Mary herself saw a definite resemblance to Prince Albert, Queen Victoria's beloved Consort, and dug out her photograph albums to prove it to her lady-in-waiting, Lady Airlie.

The names Charles, if their child was a boy, or Anne if a girl, had been chosen by Prince Philip and Princess Elizabeth some time before the birth, 'for personal and private reasons'. Some saw it as a reversion to the Stuart names that had been abandoned with the advent of the House of Hanover, but in reality, the parents simply liked those names. For Charles's christening, they added Philip, after his father, and Arthur George, the last two names of his maternal grandfather, the King.

The service itself was officiated by the Archbishop of Canterbury, Dr Geoffrey Fisher, on 16 December 1948. As the chapel at Buckingham Palace had been bombed during the war and the King could not travel to Windsor due to a severe vascular obstruction in his leg, it was decided to hold the ceremony in the White and Gold Music Room at Buckingham Palace. The golden Lily Font, used by all the descendants of Queen Victoria for their christenings, was brought up from Windsor and filled with water from the River Jordan, a royal tradition dating from the Crusades. In keeping with another tradition, Charles was dressed in the Honiton lace robes first worn by Queen Victoria's eldest child, Victoria, the Princess Royal. According to the Archbishop, Charles remained 'as quiet as a mouse' throughout the ceremony and was held by his aunt, Princess Margaret. She was the youngest sponsor, as royal godparents are called, the other seven also being close members of the family; the King and Queen, her brother, the Hon. David Bowes-Lyon, King Haakon of Norway, the Dowager Marchioness of Milford Haven (Prince Philip's august grandmother then aged eighty-five), his uncle Prince George of Greece and his cousin, Lady Brabourne. Charles received many christening presents including an historic one from Queen Mary—'a silver gilt cup & cover which George III had given to a godson in 1780 so that I gave a present from my gt. grandfather to my great grandson 168 years later.'

The midwife, Miss Helen Rowe, left the royal nurseries soon after the christening and her place was taken by two Scottish women, Mrs Helen Lightbody and Miss Mabel Anderson. Helen Lightbody, accorded the courtesy title of 'Mrs' since she was the senior of the two, had come from Barnwell where she was nanny to the Duchess of Gloucester's two boys, William and Richard. Miss Anderson can only have been astounded when her advertisement in the 'Situations Wanted' column of a nursing magazine was answered by the Lord Chamberlain's office in Buckingham Palace. She later went as nanny to Princess Anne's first child Peter.

Concern was growing for the health of King George VI and the Christmas of 1948 was spent in Buckingham Palace. He was, however, fit enough in January to go with his family to Sandringham. Like his father, the King adored the estate and was never happier than being a 'Norfolk Squire'. Nanny Lightbody knew the place, the people and their children well, having stayed there with William and Richard of Gloucester. One visitor to the royal nursery to inspect the infant Prince was the leggy, twelve-year-old daughter of Lord Fermoy. She was the Hon. Frances Roche, the daughter of the King's shooting and tennis friend and neighbour, and the future mother-in-law of that new-born baby.

The move to Clarence House came in July 1949. The alterations and redecorations took far longer than expected as the house, used as offices for the Red Cross during the War, had remained uninhabited for thirty years. During the extensive works, Prince Philip and Princess Elizabeth divided their time between their country house, Windlesham Moor, near Sunningdale in Berkshire, and Buckingham Palace. Clarence House, today the residence of Queen Elizabeth the Queen Mother, suited them well. It was very close to Princess Elizabeth's ailing father and 'next door' to Marlborough House, the home of Queen Mary; comfortable, too, with its central heating and new bathrooms. Rooms on the third floor had to be transformed into a nursery for Charles as only one incumbent of Clarence House, Queen Victoria's second son Prince Alfred, the last Duke of Edinburgh, had had children since the house was built in 1825. There, in a pretty pale-blue nursery with chintz curtains and with some of the furniture from Princess Elizabeth's old home of 145 Piccadilly—a rocking horse without a tail, and the glass-fronted display cabinet for glass and china miniatures—Nanny Lightbody took charge of the new infant.

Princess Elizabeth was spared the majority of her public duties so that she could devote most of her time to being the wife of a serving naval officer and mother to her son. In that first year, Prince Philip was given a post at the Admiralty and could walk to his office in Whitehall. But by the time Charles was one, his father was back at sea as a lieutenant aboard HMS *Chequers* and his mother had to resume her official duties. They were particularly keen that Charles should be shielded for as long as possible from the public glare, but to keep the press at bay, they agreed to be filmed with him at Windlesham Moor and to release his statistics on his first birthday: weight 24 lbs, hair gold and shiny, teeth six and pearly-white. Charles inherited his mother's love of, and collection of stuffed toys on wheels, and at the age of one he could walk with the aid of a fluffy blue elephant on wheels.

The undivided attention of his mother and father, when he was home, and the nursery staff ended with the birth of Anne on 15 August 1950 at Clarence House. Being so close in age Charles and Anne were to grow up together in that secure and loving home. There were no pressures in the house except that their father was often away at sea. As Princess Elizabeth's days became fuller, so the need grew for a strict discipline in the nursery. Every day, whether in London or the country, Charles and Anne were dressed at seven o'clock, then given breakfast.

7. Prince Charles at the age of two in Green Park in London with his nanny, Mabel Anderson, and police officer. Security was not as tight then as it is now.

They played until nine o'clock when they were taken down to their parents' bedrooms for half-an-hour. If fine, a trip to St James's Park followed before returning for lunch. There was always a rest in the afternoons, then another outing. Princess Elizabeth always tried to be back from her engagements in time for nursery tea and bath-time.

As has been the fate of all royal children Charles was soon separated from his parents, the first time when his mother went to join Prince Philip in Malta when he took command of his first ship, HMS *Magpie*. Charles was left in the care of his aunt, Princess Margaret, and his grandparents at Buckingham Palace. The King wrote to his daughter, 'Charles is too sweet, stumping round the room. We shall love having him at Sandringham. He is the fifth generation to live there, and I hope he will get to like the place.' The next parting was longer when Prince Philip and Princess Elizabeth went on a state visit to Canada and the United States of America. They missed Charles's third birthday but as a special treat he was allowed to meet them at Heathrow airport and switch on the landing lights.

Something happened during the next separation from his parents which was to have the most dramatic effect on Charles's early life. For some time a tour of East Africa, Australia and New Zealand had been planned for George VI and Queen Elizabeth but each time a date was fixed, the King was too ill to travel. Finally, Princess Elizabeth and Prince Philip went in their place and left for Kenya on 31 January 1952. As usual, the King and Queen took their grandchildren to Sandringham. On 5 February, Lord Fermoy was one of the many guns made up from the estate employees and tenants at the Sandringham hare shoot. It was a crisp but cold day and everyone, especially the King, enjoyed the day's shooting. Very early the next morning, however, the King died in his sleep. Princess Elizabeth returned home immediately. She was now Queen, and Charles, a little over three years old, became heir apparent to the throne.

In this capacity, Charles automatically became the Duke of Cornwall, Duke of Rothesay, Earl of Carrick and Baron of Renfrew, Lord of the Isles and Great Steward of Scotland. His new titles meant little to him although he quickly recognised his new name of Duke of Cornwall at mattins, when prayers were said for members of the Royal Family. The change in Charles's life was far greater then just his titles, although his parents made every effort to ensure otherwise. There was the same half-hour romp every morning in his parents' rooms and in order to preserve the sacred bath-time session, the Queen even asked the Prime Minister, Winston Churchill, to put back their weekly meeting by one hour so as not to clash with the event. The other change was the move to Buckingham Palace where the day and night nurseries on the second floor were redecorated to resemble, as far as possible, the ones left behind in Clarence House.

When the Queen married in 1948 she was twenty-one and her father fifty-three. Reasonably, she could have expected her father to live for another twenty to twenty-five years giving her and her husband the time and freedom to bring up their children and enjoy them to the full. Her father's early death robbed them of that time and put extra pressures on their children. The Queen shielded Charles for as long as possible, insisting that he be treated as any other little boy. Once he met a secretary in the corridor of Buckingham Palace and asked him what he was doing there. 'I'm going to see the Queen,' explained the secretary. 'Oh yes?' said Charles, 'Who's she?' When the secretary told him that she was his mother, Charles was amazed. 'It was as if I had given away the secret of Father Christmas', the secretary admitted later.

The staff at Buckingham Palace were instructed to call Charles only by his Christian name—the same went for his sister and his brothers, up to the age of eighteen, when they are addressed as 'Sir' or 'Ma'am'. However hard his parents tried to keep his life 'unroyal', Charles inevitably fell victim to his new position as heir apparent. He missed being driven by his father and instead had his own car and chauffeur. Another addition was a nursery footman, Richard Brown. When he went for a walk with Nanny Lightbody or Miss Anderson, they were shadowed by his Special Branch police officer, Sergeant Kelly. Because Charles

8. King George VI with his grandson, Charles, aged three. This photograph, taken at Buckingham Palace, is a favourite of the Queen's and stands on her desk.

began to be recognised in the parks and on the streets around Buckingham Palace, he was taken for walks in Richmond Park, on Putney Heath or on Wimbledon Common where no one would expect to see the heir to the throne.

Charles began to emerge as a good-natured boy. He adored animals and took great pride in looking after his two corgis, a hamster named Chi-Chi and a pair of South American love birds, David and Annie—named after the 'Wild West' characters Davy Crockett and Annie Oakley. Very little accurate news filtered out of the royal nursery, so it was generally assumed by the press that Charles was a rather dull little boy. Although he was beginning to look like his extrovert father and to copy his mannerisms, he took after his mother and her father in their early years by being shy and reserved. His solemn features and his tendency to shrink from the public gaze, in contrast to his sister, gave entirely the wrong impression of his character, for he was a docile child, although given to violent outbursts of temper that were immediately followed by effusive and embarrassed apologies. Just as these outbursts were typical of his antecedents, so was a particular brand of humour, the practical joke, usually made at someone else's expense. Charles enjoyed these pranks enormously and practised them with relish—like the time he slipped an ice-cube down the neck of an unsuspecting footman. He was punished just like any other naughty boy. His nanny and nursery maid were not above spanking him when he stepped out of line, and occasionally his father would spank him for more serious infringements, like the time when he put out his tongue at the crowd in the Mall or when he put a well-sucked sweet into his mother's palm just before she left the car to meet some dignitary.

At four-and-a-half years old, Charles was considered adult enough to attend his mother's Coronation but not for the whole ceremony. As Duke of Cornwall, he was the senior peer of the Realm and by tradition should have led his fellow-peers in the oath of allegiance. But his track record in public—for instance fidgeting and dropping his prayer book in church and chattering throughout a children's concert—was poor and it was decided he was not up to it and would be another worry to his mother. On Coronation Day, 2 June 1953, Charles, dressed in a silk suit and his hair slicked down with brilliantine, was escorted into a side door of Westminster Abbey by a Grenadier Guards officer and Nanny Lightbody. He stood between the Queen Mother and Princess Margaret on a footstool and watched the magnificent ceremony of the crowning of his mother. He chattered to his grandmother and offered her his hand, telling her to smell the brilliantine he had wiped from his head. After a while, Nanny Lightbody led him out through the side door and back to Buckingham Palace where he watched the rest of the ceremony and the procession on black-and-white television. On his mother's return. Charles had his first taste of public adulation for the monarchy when he joined the Queen on the balcony of the palace. He was to experience the scene many times, not least of course after his own wedding twenty-eight years later.

In November 1953, the Queen and Prince Philip embarked on their long-awaited Commonwealth Tour to Australia and New Zealand. Charles had just

9. A pensive Prince Charles, at his mother's Coronation in Westminster Abbey, stands between the Queen Mother and Princess Margaret in the Royal Box on 2 June 1953.

had his fifth birthday when his parents left for Jamaica on the first stage of their tour. It was a small consolation to Charles for being parted from his parents for six months that he and Anne were allowed to sail in the Royal Yacht *Britannia* to meet them in Tobruk. It took a week to sail to Malta where they stayed for a further week with their uncle, Lord Mountbatten, then Commander-in-Chief of the Mediterranean Fleet.

The Queen and Prince Philip were finally united with their children on board the Royal Yacht at Tobruk on 2 May. They were impressed at how much Charles had grown up in the six months they had been apart and they had much to catch up on once they were at sea for their holiday. On the last leg home, they stopped at Gibraltar before returning to England and a triumphant welcome. Their return to London marked the end of the first stage of Charles's life. His education now started in earnest.

The Queen was adamant that, as far as possible, he should be treated as any other boy of his age. To start him off on this course the Queen had interviewed and engaged a Scotswoman, Miss Catherine Peebles, who had come from teaching the Duchess of Kent's two youngest children, Alexandra and Michael.

'Mispy', as she was called, was middle-aged, diminutive and alert with no formal training, but with her calm temperament she was ideally suited to the job before her. Charles was not the easiest of pupils. In some ways he was advanced for his age having been brought up almost exclusively in contact with adults, mostly women, his father being away much of the time. On the other hand, he was a nervous, somewhat touchy child and Mispy told the Queen, 'he liked being amused rather than amusing himself . . . he was very responsive to kindness, but if you raised your voice to him, he would draw back into his shell and for a time you would be able to do nothing with him.' Competition was thought to be bad for Charles so he was allowed to go at his own pace in a class of one. The 'school' timetable was relaxed, too, and Charles was still able to enjoy the half-hour with his mother before going up to the schoolroom for lessons until midday. Lessons started with a Bible story, then a selection of history, geography, reading and writing—or arithmetic, the family failing, which he too found the most difficult. Before Mispy arrived he could just about write his name in block capitals, count to a hundred and tell the time. Now he quickly learnt to read and after the first year added French to his curriculum. The afternoons were spent with Mispy on educational visits and walks to museums, to the Tower of London or just to places of interest like Highgate Hill to give the story of Dick Whittington with his cat greater depth. These excursions into the outside world were soon to be curtailed by the ubiquitous press which quickly latched onto the routine. The Queen, through her Press Secretary, made an appeal to let her son move around the capital in peace. The pursuit was called off for a short time but it was not long before the press hounds were trailing him again, and only nature walks in Richmond Park became safe. Once, however, Charles managed to go on the Underground but fortunately he was taken for the son of Mispy and his Special Branch Police Officer.

Although the Queen had the responsibilities and work load of her office, she could relax during the holidays at Sandringham and Windsor and Balmoral in the summer, when all her family could be together with less interference from outside. Both the Queen and Queen Elizabeth the Queen Mother are great countrywomen and have passed on to Charles their love of nature and the outdoors. The Queen encouraged him to ride but it was Anne who showed greater ability and Charles soon lost interest. Later, when he took up polo under his father's aegis, he renewed his interest in horses and went on to steeplechase and hunt. Prince Philip was, according to Mabel Anderson, the under-nanny, a 'marvellous father. When the children were younger, he always used to set aside time to read to them, or help them to put together those little model toys'. It was Anne who was the more practical of the two; Charles was 'all fingers and thumbs'.

The next stage of Charles's education was to learn to integrate with children of his own age. Various children of his parents' friends' would be asked to tea and to play with Charles and the ones he liked the best would be asked more often than the others. He certainly enjoyed these visits, particularly in the country,

10. Prince Charles and his sister, Princess Anne, stopped off at Malta to stay with their great-uncle and aunt, Lord and Lady Mountbatten, on their way to meet the Queen and Prince Philip at the end of their 1953–4 Commonwealth Tour. The Royal Yacht *Britannia* is in the background.

but it was no substitute for actually having to make his own friends. Also, he was beginning to outgrow Mispy's schoolroom and was ready for proper lessons. In 1956, when Charles was nearly eight, the Queen and Prince Philip asked Colonel Henry Townend to tea at Buckingham Palace. Colonel Townend was the founder and headmaster of Hill House, a smart pre-preparatory school in Knightsbridge. Over tea it was agreed that Charles would continue his lessons in the morning with Mispy, then join the boys for games in the afternoon until he became accustomed to being with them and they with him. The experiment worked in so far as Charles met new people, although he showed little promise on the football field.

The first stage of integration complete, Charles was sent to the school for lessons on 28 January 1957. He arrived with Mispy dressed in the rust and deep-gold uniform of Hill House. The boys, themselves mostly from privileged backgrounds, were told to treat Charles like any other pupil, and the first day passed off without a hitch. Charles was excited as he told his parents that night of his first day and for their part they were happy that their son might after all lead a normal life.

The Queen's initial optimism was dashed the next day when Colonel Townend telephoned to say that his school was under siege, not only from the press but also from the local residents. Charles arrived half-an-hour late that morning and scurried, highly embarrassed, past the sightseers and a barrage of cameras. The next day, the Queen kept him at home until her Press Secretary had contacted all the 'guilty' editors of the papers covering Charles's new school and they called off their reporters. From then on, he was able to enjoy the rest of the term, apart from a period of three weeks in bed with tonsilitis.

The motto of Hill House was taken from Plutarch, 'A boy's mind is not a vessel to be filled, but a fire to be kindled.' In Charles's case, the school lived up to its motto and by the end of the summer term he had advanced significantly in the classroom and had benefited from the school's moral code. Although he was thought of very much as a plodder in his work, Charles was keen on his favourite sports, swimming and wrestling, and showed great promise with his painting.

That summer of 1957, Charles had his first taste of sailing with his father at Cowes on the Isle of Wight, an experience that started with sea-sickness but ended with an appreciation of the sea and the joys to be had from sailing. However, when the Royal Family then made their annual pilgrimage to Balmoral, Charles became quiet and thoughtful, dreading the fact that he would soon be leaving the security and comfort of home for a boarding preparatory school.

For some months, the Queen and Prince Philip had sought advice from friends and visited many different types of schools to find the most suitable for Charles. In the end, they decided on Cheam, not just because Prince Philip had gone there but because it was far enough from London and the disruptive influence of the press, and they liked the joint headmasters, Peter Beck and Mark Wheeler, and the school itself. Charles had already visited Cheam, an attractive Georgian house close to the Berkshire village of Headly, with his parents and Anne.

11. Before a polo match at Windsor Great Park, Prince Charles talks to one of his father's polo ponies.

12. The Queen and Prince Philip were among the spectators who watched Prince Charles bowl during the Field Day of his prep school, Hill House, 8 July 1957

Charles took the overnight train to London with his parents, then was driven the sixty miles by his father in his Lagonda to the school at the start of the Michaelmas term, 1957. A letter had been sent to all parents during the summer:

> It is the wish of the Queen and Prince Philip that there shall be no alteration in the way the school is run and that Prince Charles is to be treated the same as other boys ... It will be a great help if you will explain this. His parents' wishes are that he should be given exactly the same education and upbringing as the other boys at the school.

The dreaded moment came when his parents drove away and left Charles behind. He was one of the youngest boys in the school, knew nobody and did not have that inbred schoolboy quality of being able to make friends. When the mathematics master who had been instructed to look after Charles eventually found him, he saw a forlorn boy, 'much in need of a haircut', standing on his own and shunned by the other boys. The misery, however, did not last for too long and Charles soon found his feet. Subconsciously, Charles had, and by his own admission still has, a horror of befriending the wrong people and in those early days at Cheam he found that friends were reticent in coming forward in case they were thought to be 'sucking up' to the heir to the throne.

Considering his background, Charles settled down to the life at Cheam well. In subjects that interested him, like history or geography, he did well, while those he failed to understand—mathematics, Latin and Greek—he found very difficult. At games, he did better in individual rather than team sports, continuing to be an enthusiastic performer in the gymnasium and in the swimming pool.

While Charles's life continued within the school along the lines of any other pupil, the press were still active outside. Stories about him appeared almost daily, most of them totally apocryphal. Reports that the staff and pupils were selling stories about Charles soured the atmosphere of the school and the Queen's worst fears were confirmed. During the Christmas holidays, the editors of all national newspapers were once again called to Buckingham Palace and told in the strongest possible terms to keep away from the school and to print only stories of 'a genuine significance'. If they did not heed the warning, then Prince Charles would be taken away and educated privately. Finally, the press agreed and Charles continued his school career more or less uninterrupted.

13. Robert Whitby escorts Prince Philip and Prince Charles to Charles's house on the first day of the summer term 1962 at Gordonstoun in Scotland.

The title of Prince of Wales is an honorary one, granted by the sovereign to the eldest son and heir. At the age of nine, on 26 July 1958, the Queen created Charles Prince of Wales and with that title he automatically became a Knight of the Garter and the Earl of Chester. The Queen was to have announced it herself at the closing ceremony of the Commonwealth Games in Cardiff but she could not attend because of a minor operation and Prince Philip took her place. However, a recording of her intended speech was played over the loud speakers:

I want to take this opportunity of speaking to all Welsh people, not only in this arena, but wherever they may be. The British Empire and Commonwealth Games in the capital, together with all the activities of the Festival of Wales, have made this a memorable year for the principality. I have therefore decided to mark it further by an act which will, I hope, give as much pleasure to all Welshmen as it does to me. I intend to create my son Charles Prince of Wales.

The announcement was greeted with a tremendous cheer, then every voice in the stadium of Cardiff Arms Park broke into 'God Bless the Prince of Wales'. The message continued: 'When he is grown up, I will present him to you at Caernarvon.' The Investiture of the Prince of Wales took place as promised on 1 July 1969 at Caernarvon Castle.

The headmaster of Cheam, Mr Beck, had been warned by the Queen of her announcement and he arranged for Charles and a few other boys to watch the ceremony. Although Charles already knew of the honour, he shrank from the involuntary applause in the room. He recalled years later in an interview,

> I remember being acutely embarrassed when it was announced. I heard this marvellous great cheer coming from the stadium in Cardiff, and for a little boy of nine it was rather bewildering. All the others turned and looked at me in amazement. It perhaps didn't mean all that much to me then; later on, as I grew older, it became apparent what it meant.

Although Charles was basically not a complex boy, he did have trouble balancing his two worlds—on the one hand becoming increasingly aware of his position as heir to the throne, on the other being simply a prep-school boy. He was not naturally gifted and his headmaster summed him up as being 'above average in intelligence but only average in attainment'. In matters he could directly relate to his position and family, such as current affairs, history and geography, he was far ahead of his contemporaries, but in the main he was less mature than his fellow-pupils and remained so for the next ten years.

A royal ploy to conquer shyness is to perform on stage. Charles's chance came in the school play *The Last Baron* when the boy playing the lead part fell ill. Charles, his understudy, stepped in and gave a creditable performance as the Duke of Gloucester [later to become King Richard III]. The *Cheam School Chronicle* gave it a good review: 'Prince Charles played the traditional Gloucester with competence and depth: he had a good voice and excellent elocution, and very well conveyed the ambition and bitterness of the twisted hunchback.' His parents, however, were not in the audience, for that very night the Queen gave birth to her second son and third child, Andrew. Although the school was given a day's holiday to celebrate the birth, Charles was not allowed home to see his brother until the end of term. The wedding of his aunt. Princess Margaret, to Antony Armstrong-Jones, was different and Charles attended the ceremony at Westminster Abbey and the wedding breakfast afterwards at Buckingham Palace.

When Charles left Cheam at the end of the Lent term, 1962, it was with an undistinguished sporting and academic record, but he was remembered with much affection by the staff. 'Most of the time he was very quiet. He never spoke out of turn. Sometimes his voice was so low that it was difficult to hear him. But he was a boy who preferred action to noise. When there was a task to do, he got on with it quietly. No fuss.' Where his father had shone on the Cheam games field, Charles was very much second-best. He hated rugger and was bored by cricket, although he occasionally made the First XI. His captaincy of the First XI soccer team was a disaster—they lost every match, scoring just four goals against eighty-two, a record that earned him a mild reprimand in the *Cheam School Chronicle*: 'At centre half, Prince Charles seldom drove himself as hard as his ability and position demanded.' Charles did pass his Common Entrance Examination although the school that had been chosen for him, Gordonstoun, did not require it. The Queen and Prince Philip decided that he should take the examination anyway, not only to deter critics who might say that he was so backward that Gordonstoun was the only school that would take him, but as a measure of self-satisfaction for Charles as well.

There had been a great family debate as to where Charles should go after Cheam. The Queen and the Queen Mother both favoured Eton but Prince Philip would not hear of it. It was too close to the comfort of Windsor Castle and the Queen Mother's house, Royal Lodge, which would have been 'in bounds' every week-end. As the school is spread out all over the town, the boys in their distinctive dress have to walk through the streets between classrooms and their houses, and Charles would thus be prey to the cameras of curious tourists and endless pressmen. Also, Prince Philip considered the school too élitist. Other schools were considered but none had all the advantages of Gordonstoun. Besides being Prince Philip's old school, where he had enjoyed his time, it was also far enough away on the shore of the Moray Firth in the north of Scotland to be out of reach of Fleet Street. The school was also tough enough and, because of the fee structure, cosmopolitan enough to silence the critics who thought Charles's education too tame and restricted.

Gordonstoun was modelled on Salem, a school run by its founder, Dr Kurt Hahn, in Germany. After the rise of Nazism, the Jewish headmaster was forced to leave and fled to Scotland in 1933 with thirty of his pupils, one of whom was in fact Prince Philip. The theme of Gordonstoun's motto, *Plus est en vous* (There is more in you) was, and still is, rigorously applied to all pupils. Hahn believed that self-reliance and self-confidence were the prime factors for a good citizen and that these could only be achieved through a high degree of fitness. Another way of promoting his pupils to their best was through community service. The boys manned the school's fire brigade, coastguard station, mountain and ocean rescue teams and, over the years, have been responsible for the saving of many lives.

It was worse for Charles arriving at Gordonstoun with his father for the summer term of 1962 than arriving at Cheam for his last term. There he had reached a position of some seniority, having worked his way up the school ladder to Monitor (prefect). On that May Day, he was back on the bottom rung, in hostile surroundings and friendless. Father and son were welcomed by the headmaster, Robert Chew, and Charles was taken to his house, Windmill Lodge, and introduced to his housemaster, Robert Whitby. The dormitories had changed little since Prince Philip's day and Charles shared the soulless room with its unpainted walls and bare, splintery floorboards with fifty-nine of the 400 pupils. Among those pupils were three of his second cousins, Norton Knatchbull, Lord Louis Mountbatten's grandson, Prince Welf of Hanover and Prince Alexander of Yugoslavia, but when they tried to befriend the royal new-boy, they were put off by their contemporaries who accused them of trying to ingratiate themselves with the heir to the throne. As the term progressed, Charles's position did not improve for, as an ex-pupil told a Sunday newspaper, 'How can you treat a boy as just an ordinary chap when his mother's portrait is on the coins you spend in the school shop, on the stamps you put on your letters home, and when a detective follows him wherever he goes? Most boys tend to fight shy of friendship with Charles. The result is that he is very lonely. It is this loneliness, rather than the school's toughness, which must be hardest on him.'

For the whole school, the daily routine was indeed arduous. By the time the boys sat down to breakfast at 8.15 am, they had been woken at 7 am by the 'waker', a boy ringing a bell; gone for a run in the garden wearing, whatever the weather, only a pair of shorts and gym-shoes; dressed after a wash and a cold shower; and made their beds and cleaned their shoes. After breakfast, where the juniors waited at the tables, there were morning prayers and the rest of the day was spent exactly as the headmaster, Mr Chew set out in his timetable:

9.10 Classwork begins. There are five 40-minute periods in the morning for every boy. One of these, on several days a week, is a training break (running, jumping, discus and javelin throwing, assault course, etc.) under the Physical Training Master.

1.20 Lunch. After lunch there is a rest period (20 minutes): music or reading aloud to boys relaxing on their backs.

2.30 Afternoon activities. On three days a week there are either games (rugger or hockey in winter; cricket, lawn tennis or athletics in summer), or seamanship or practical work on the estate. The proportion of time spent on each depends upon a boy's interests and development. One afternoon a week is allocated to the Services: Coast Guard Watchers, Sea Cadets, Army Cadets, Scouts, Fire Service, Mountain Rescue and Surf Life Saving. One afternoon and evening a week are given to work on boys' individual projects which are exhibited and judged at the end of each year. On Saturday afternoons there are matches and opportunities for expeditions.

4.00 Warm wash and cold shower. Change into evening school uniform. Tea. After tea, classes or tutorial periods.

6.20 Supper, followed by preparation in Houses or by 'Societies'.

9.15 Bedtime: silence period of five minutes.

9.30 lights out.

14. Formal portrait of Prince Charles shortly before his fourteenth birthday in 1962.

In those rare moments that Charles had to himself he was wary of accepting too many privileged invitations which would alienate him still further from his fellow-pupils. Occasionally he went to shoot or to dine with the Lord Lieutenant of the County, Captain Ian Tennant, and his wife, Lady Margaret Tennant. There was also the land agent, or factor, of Balmoral with whom he could stay for the odd weekend, but best of all, Charles could stay with his grandmother, the Queen Mother, at Birkhall, whenever she came up to stay. She helped him considerably through that miserable period of loneliness.

The press were asked once again to respect the Queen's wishes by leaving her son alone and allowing his school to function normally. However, they considered that the holidays were fair game. Shortly before his fourteenth birthday, Charles shot his first stag and the furore that followed in the press from anti-field sports societies went on for weeks. When he went to ski in Bavaria with Prince Ludwig of Hesse, the throng of pressmen was so vast that they had to retire to the Prince's private slopes. Charles made an excellent start at skiing and has progressed steadily to become a proficient skier today.

As Charles advanced up the complicated system of seniority at Gordonstoun, he became more used to the system and the reticence of his fellow-pupils and so disliked the place less. This improvement in his lot was reflected in his much improved school reports. He also began to make friends, being accepted as an individual rather than shunned as an outsider.

As part of his promotion to the Junior Training Plan, he was included in an expedition to the Outer Hebrides on the school's yacht *Pinta* on 17 June 1963. They berthed at Stornaway on the Isle of Lewis and went ashore to the Crown Hotel while Donald Green, Charles's police officer, went to buy tickets for the cinema that evening. While he was gone, a crowd gathered outside the hotel window, all jostling for a better view. Years later Charles recalled the occasion:

> I thought, 'I can't bear this any more', and went off somewhere else. The only other place was the bar. Having never been into a bar before, the first thing I thought of doing was having a drink, of course. And being terrified, not knowing what to do, I said the first drink that came into my head, which happened to be cherry brandy, because I had drunk it before when it was cold out shooting. Hardly had I taken a sip when the whole world exploded around my ears.

The 'explosion' was caused by a female freelance journalist, dubbed 'that dreadful woman' by Charles, who caught him drinking alcohol, under age, in the bar. The story made world headlines, with dire results. Charles lost his position and privileges as a member of the Junior Training Plan and Donald Green resigned from the police force after a severe reprimand from his superior.

The press were also responsible for another scandal, this time involving the theft of one of Charles's exercise books. The book contained four of his essays and was stolen from the classroom, sold outside the school and finally ended up in a Lancashire newspaper office where it was recovered by the police, but not before xerox copies were being processed by the German magazine *Der Stern*, the

French *Paris-Match* and the American *Time-Life Magazine*. The essays were published in full and in fact Charles came out of the affair with credit. His form-master's comment of the work, 'Quite well argued', was also published, a comment that most readers agreed was fair for a boy of nearly sixteen. Charles had sat for seven 'O' levels and passed five of them, English Language and literature, history, French and Latin, but failed mathematics and physics. He retook mathematics the following year and passed.

The higher that Charles rose in the Gordonstoun system, the more opportunities to develop skills and interests opened up to him. Also his self-confidence grew. He gained his life-saving certificates partnered by his cousin Prince Welf, joined the Army section of the Combined Cadet Force and spent some time at HMS *Vernon*, a Royal Navy training camp near Portsmouth, his first taste of the Senior Service. He also developed an interest in archaeology, working on digs close to the school—an interest which expanded into anthropology, the two subjects he read when he went up to Cambridge University.

Of all his achievements at Gordonstoun, perhaps Charles's portrayal of Macbeth, shortly after his seventeenth birthday, is the one best remembered. For once, he eclipsed his father, for Prince Philip in the same play thirty years before had only been selected for the minor part of an attendant lord, Donablain, and that was more for his riding than acting skill. The Queen and Prince Philip did attend this performance and, in deference to the Queen, the producer deleted the stage direction, 'Enter Macduff with Macbeth's head'. Charles's parents were impressed with his performance, as was the *Gordonstoun Record*:

> Prince Charles was at his very best in the quiet poetic soliloquies, the poetry of which he so beautifully brought out, and in the bits which expressed Macbeth's terrible agony of remorse and fear. In the second part of the play, he equally expressed the degenerative hardening of Macbeth's character, the assumption of cynicism in an attempt to blunt the underlying and too painful moral sensitivity.

Besides acting, music was very much part of Charles's life. He abandoned the piano in favour of the trumpet, but only after terrible complaints from the German music mistress. Later, he took up the cello after seeing Jacqueline Du Pré play at the Festival Hall, an interest that gave him great pleasure but was to lapse through lack of time during his Cambridge days.

By the Christmas holidays of 1965, Charles now aged seventeen, found the routine and the life at Gordonstoun restricting. He wanted a break and after much deliberation and consultation with the Australian High Commissioner in London, it was decided that he should go to Australia to spend a term at a branch of the Geelong Church of England Grammar School, Timbertop, in the State of Victoria.

He left for Australia in January 1966 feeling rather homesick; 'it was a very sad moment, of course, leaving England, seeing one's father and sister standing on the tarmac and waving goodbye but I found the moment I was in the air it

15. A keen naturalist, Prince Charles visits a bird colony at Upolu Cay in Queensland, Australia after spending two terms at Timbertop in 1966.

1. Prince Charles, just nineteen weeks old, with his parents, Princess Elizabeth and
Prince Philip, at Buckingham Palace, 1949.

2. Even aged seven, Prince Charles was a frequent visitor to Windsor Great Park to watch his father play polo.

3. Prince Charles, aged fourteen, and Princess Anne at the Braemar Gathering, September 1962.

4. Prince Charles with his polo ponies in Windsor Great Park, August 1965.

5. Diana Spencer at the age of seven with her brother, Charles, aged four, in 1968.

6. The thirteen-year-old Diana Spencer on her mother and step-father's farm, Ardencaple, on the Isle of Seil, Argyllshire, Scotland, 1974.

7. Lady Diana Spencer, sixteen, at a nightclub in Chateau d'Oex with friends from her finishing school, Institut Alpin Videmanette, Switzerland, 1977.

was much better.' Prince Philip had sent his Equerry, Squadron-Leader David Checketts, to look after his son and it was he who summed up the success of the Australian part of Charles's education; 'I went out there with a boy, and returned with a man'. The transformation during those seven months (the original one term was extended to two followed by a quick tour of the country) was particularly noticed by those who knew him, not least by Charles himself.

When he returned, as promised, to Gordonstoun to take his 'A' levels in History and French he was elected by his house, Windmill, a helper—the equivalent of head of house, and the following term the headmaster chose him as guardian, or head-boy, of the school. During the summer term 1967, when Charles was eighteen-and-a-half, he passed his two 'A' levels, one of them, History with distinction—enough to qualify him for Cambridge University.

Charles was happy to leave school but was glad he had gone to Gordonstoun:

> The toughness of the place is too much exaggerated by report. It was the character of the general education there—Kurt Hahn's principles; an education which tried to balance the physical and mental with the emphasis on self-reliance to develop a rounded human being. I did not enjoy school as much as I might have, but that was because I am happier at home than anywhere else. But Gordonstoun developed my will-power and self-control, helped me to discipline myself, and I think that discipline, not in the sense of making you bath in cold water, but in the Latin sense—giving shape and form and tidiness to your life—is the most important thing your education can do.

Perhaps the most pertinent comment on Charles's character as he launched into manhood came from his former headmaster of Geelong, Thomas Garnett: 'leaving aside the question of Royalty, we have really enjoyed having Prince Charles at our school. Before his visit, most Australians had very hazy, and possibly erroneous ideas about him, if they had any ideas at all. They probably thought of him just as a distant, uninteresting figurehead. In future most of them will know him as a friendly, intelligent, natural boy with a good sense of humour, someone who by no means has an easy task ahead of him in life.'

Throughout the whole of Charles's childhood and education, he was the 'royal guinea-pig'. There were no precedents for him to follow, like his two younger brothers after him, and it was only through his dogged determination to succeed, that he won through at the very end. The lessons of his own childhood were well learned and, by his own admission, have formed the basis of his life today. Charles was brought up within a close-knit and happy family and it is that atmosphere that he will recreate in his own family, now that he is a father.

2

Diana

One night in February 1977, a group of girls at a finishing school met in their French mistress's room. Four years later, that same French mistress was to recall their conversation: 'We discussed life in general and what the girls wanted to do. Diana was very broad-minded, but she was also very idealistic about what she wanted for herself. She knew she wanted to work with children—and then she wanted to get married and have children of her own.' The school was the Institut Alpin Videmanette at Chateau d'Oex in the Swiss Alps and Diana was then Lady Diana Spencer, the future Princess of Wales. None of them, least of all her, could possibly have believed that she would achieve those three aims in life, to care for children, marry and have her first baby, all in a little over five years. More unbelievable then, though in retrospect perhaps not surprising, was that she would 'contract' a *royal* marriage and give birth to an heir to the throne. Although born a commoner, she is now firmly a member of the Royal Family and in that capacity, as the latest royal mother, she is included in these pages along with the other royal children. Her own childhood is especially interesting when compared to that of her husband.

The Princess of Wales was born the Honourable Diana Spencer late on the sunny afternoon of Saturday 1 July 1961. The birth took place in the very same room in which her mother, the Viscountess Althorp, had been born twenty-five years before, for her parents, Lord and Lady Fermoy, had also lived at Park House, on the Sandringham estate in Norfolk. The baby's father was Edward John, Viscount Althorp, heir to the 7th Earl Spencer.

The confinement through those last sweltering days of June had been trouble-free and the birth uncomplicated. According to Lord Althorp, the baby, who weighed 7 lb 12 oz, was a 'superb physical specimen'. Lord and Lady Althorp already had two daughters, Sarah aged six and Jane aged four. Their son and heir, Charles, was born three years later.

The proud parents had married at Westminster Abbey on 1 June 1954; it was a glittering wedding officiated by a family friend, the Right Reverend Percy Herbert, Bishop of Norwich. Although retired as bishop, he now returned to the little parish church at Sandringham to christen the baby—Diana Frances; Diana

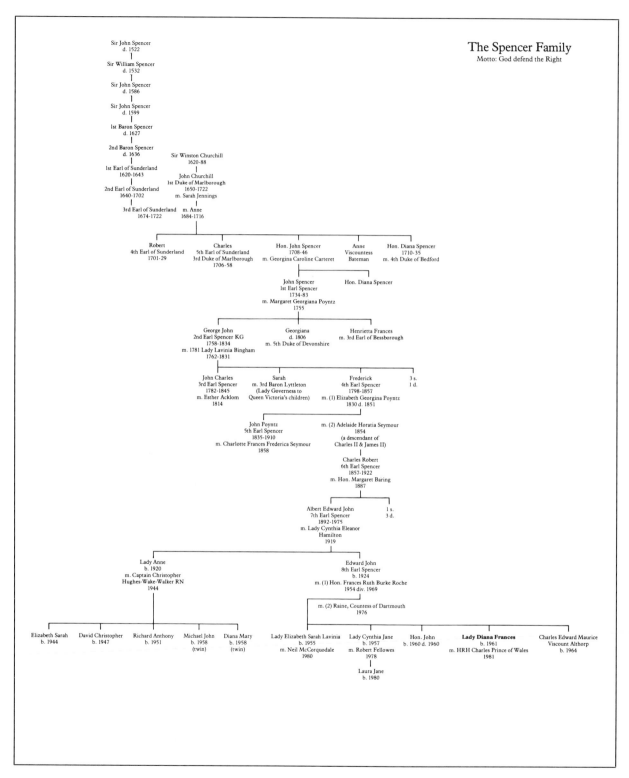

The Spencer Family
Motto: God defend the Right

Sir John Spencer
d. 1522

Sir William Spencer
d. 1532

Sir John Spencer
d. 1586

Sir John Spencer
d. 1599

1st Baron Spencer
d. 1627

2nd Baron Spencer
d. 1636

1st Earl of Sunderland
1620-1643

Sir Winston Churchill
1620-88

2nd Earl of Sunderland
1640-1702

John Churchill
1st Duke of Marlborough
1650-1722
m. Sarah Jennings

3rd Earl of Sunderland
1674-1722

m. Anne
1684-1716

Robert	Charles	Hon. John Spencer	Anne	Hon. Diana Spencer
4th Earl of Sunderland	5th Earl of Sunderland	1708-46	Viscountess	1710-35
1701-29	3rd Duke of Marlborough	m. Georgina Caroline Carteret	Bateman	m. 4th Duke of Bedford
	1706-58			

John Spencer
1st Earl Spencer
1734-83
m. Margaret Georgiana Poyntz
1755

Hon. Diana Spencer

George John	Georgiana	Henrietta Frances
2nd Earl Spencer KG	d. 1806	m. 3rd Earl of Bessborough
1758-1834	m. 5th Duke of Devonshire	
m. 1781 Lady Lavinia Bingham		
1762-1831		

John Charles	Sarah	Frederick	3 s.
3rd Earl Spencer	m. 3rd Baron Lyttleton	4th Earl Spencer	1 d.
1782-1845	(Lady Governess to	1798-1857	
m. Esther Acklom	Queen Victoria's children)	m. (1) Elizabeth Georgina Poyntz	
1814		1830 d. 1851	

John Poyntz
5th Earl Spencer
1835-1910
m. Charlotte Frances Frederica Seymour
1858

m. (2) Adelaide Horatia Seymour
1854
(a descendant of
Charles II & James II)

Charles Robert
6th Earl Spencer
1857-1922
m. Hon. Margaret Baring
1887

Albert Edward John	1 s.
7th Earl Spencer	3 d.
1892-1975	
m. Lady Cynthia Eleanor	
Hamilton	
1919	

Lady Anne	Edward John
b. 1920	8th Earl Spencer
m. Captain Christopher	b. 1924
Hughes-Wake-Walker RN	m. (1) Hon. Frances Ruth Burke Roche
1944	1954 div. 1969

m. (2) Raine, Countess of Dartmouth
1976

Elizabeth Sarah	David Christopher	Richard Anthony	Michael John	Diana Mary	Lady Elizabeth Sarah Lavinia	Lady Cynthia Jane	Hon. John	**Lady Diana Frances**	Charles Edward Maurice
b. 1944	b. 1947	b. 1951	b. 1958	b. 1958	b. 1955	b. 1957	b. 1960 d. 1960	b. 1961	Viscount Althorp
			(twin)	(twin)	m. Neil McCorquodale	m. Robert Fellowes		m. HRH Charles Prince of Wales	b. 1964
					1980	1978		1981	

Laura Jane
b. 1980

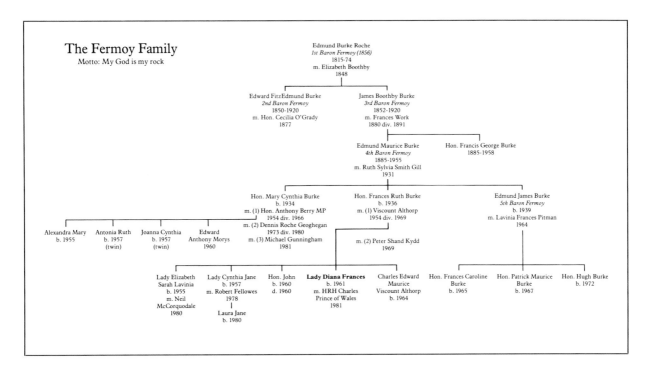

after two Spencer ancestresses, and Frances after her mother. Her godparents were chosen from close friends and Norfolk neighbours—Alexander Gilmour, John Floyd, Carol Fox, who lived at Anmer Hall, now the home of the Duke and Duchess of Kent, and Lady Mary Colman, a Bowes-Lyon niece of the Queen Mother's and wife of the Lord Lieutenant of Norfolk.

Although Diana's roots are firmly in Norfolk, her family's association with that county are a mere sixty years old. They began with her maternal grandfather, Maurice Roche. He and his identical twin Francis were brought up in America and when Maurice, the older child by twenty minutes, succeeded to the title of Fermoy as fourth baron in 1920, they returned to England. The barony itself, however, dates from 1856 when Edmund Burke Roche was created Baron Fermoy for his services as a Member of Parliament for County Cork in Ireland. The family were originally Welsh, for their ancestor, Adam de Rupe of Roch Castle in Pembrokeshire, went with the mercenary force under Richard of Clare, Earl of Pembroke and Stiguil, better known as 'Strongbow', on his invasion of Ireland in the twelfth century and settled there. The first Lord Fermoy's grandson, James, married an American heiress, the daughter of Frances Work of New York and it is through this American connection that Diana happens to be seventh cousin to both Humphrey Bogart and Rudolf Valentino.

As an Irish peer, Maurice, Lord Fermoy, was eligible to sit in the House of Commons and was eventually elected as the Member of Parliament for King's Lynn, a seat he was to hold from 1924 to 1936 and again for two years during the Second World War. At the age of forty-six, he met the daughter of another twin,

Ruth Sylvia Gill from Aberdeenshire, and married her in 1931, the year he was also elected Mayor of King's Lynn. As a friend of King George V and Queen Mary, he was granted the lease of Park House, a large and commodious Victorian house within the immediate grounds of their beloved Norfolk home, Sandringham House. They were not neighbours for long, for the King died in January 1936, the very day that the Fermoys' second daughter, Frances Ruth Burke Roche, was born. Queen Mary was able to tell the King the news of her birth just before he died.

This happy association with the Royal Family was to continue, for King George VI, and his wife Queen Elizabeth, had much in common with the Fermoys. They shared a love of the country, especially the county of Norfolk. Both the King and Lord Fermoy were excellent tennis players and good shots. Their wives, both from the east coast of Scotland, became devoted friends. Lady Fermoy was appointed first an Extra Woman of the Bedchamber, then Woman of the Bedchamber, and is now Lady-in-Waiting to the Queen Mother. Both women share a love of music and Lady Fermoy is especially remembered in King's Lynn as the founder of their festival. When the Prince of Wales and Lady Diana Spencer became engaged, their respective grandmothers were thrilled and proud of the part they both played in the engagement.

Lord and Lady Fermoy provided a secure and happy home for their children. Besides Frances, there was an elder sister, Mary, and a younger brother, Edmund. Their life in the nursery and schoolroom of Park House was identical to the one enjoyed by Diana and her sisters and brother. It was an active life, one spent mostly outdoors with friends on the Sandringham or neighbouring estates. There was always plenty to do with their horses and dogs, bicycles and childrens' parties, and occasionally they were allowed to go to the miniature dairy made by Queen Alexandra for her children and grandchildren.

School was taken slightly more seriously. Lessons were held in the schoolroom of Park House with some of the children of the Fermoys' friends, under the governess Miss Gertrude Allen, with the sobriquet of 'Gert'. When Frances and her sister graduated from the schoolroom they went to Downham, a smart school in Hertfordshire. Frances did exceptionally well, leaving at the age of sixteen as head girl and captain of cricket, netball, lacrosse and tennis. With her father's coaching, she became a good tennis player and although she qualified for a national school's tournament, appendicitis robbed her of the chance to play at Wimbledon.

Soon after Frances left school in 1952, she met again one of the equerries to the young Queen, Captain, the Viscount Althorp—Johnny to his family and friends. He had been a regular visitor to Sandringham as he had been equerry for two years to the late King George VI. Being a Spencer and heir to the Earldom and estates, Johnny was one of the most eligible bachelors of the day. The Spencers have been inextricably linked by service and blood ties with the English sovereign since before the Norman Conquest but the family fortunes stem from the early sixteenth century when a Sir John Spencer bought two manors,

Wormleighton in Warwickshire and Althorp in Northamptonshire. From then on, the Spencers have been prominent as statesmen and politicians, courtiers, farmers and above all, collectors of art and literature, and their family seat, Althorp, 'remains as a testimonial to all those Spencers who not only gave their time and energies in public service, but managed to add their own special contribution to the house'. It is through these Spencer ancestors that Diana claims 'kinship' with the Prince of Wales, being eleventh cousin once removed from James 1, and both of them having a common ancestor in Henry VII. Another link is through the third Duke of Devonshire, but more directly they are related through the children of King Charles II and three of his mistresses and through his brother, King James II and his mistress, Arabella Churchill.

For her Commonwealth Tour of Australia and New Zealand in 1954, the Queen chose Lord Althorp as her Master of the Household. When they left for the six-month visit, he and Frances Roche were unofficially engaged. They wrote to each other every day and their engagement proper was announced while he was in Australia. When the Royal party reached Tobruk on the way home, Johnny was allowed to return to London to prepare for his wedding, which was held in Westminster Abbey. At the age of eighteen, Frances was the youngest bride to marry there this century. The Queen and Prince Philip, the Queen Mother and Princess Margaret were among 1,500 guests at the Abbey and afterwards at the reception in St James's Palace.

The Althorps set up their married home in Gloucestershire where Lord Althorp was a student on the one-year farming course at the Royal Agricultural College, Cirencester. Their first daughter, Sarah, was born on 19 March 1955, just ten-and-a-half months after their wedding. They were happy in Gloucestershire but after the first year, Lady Althorp's father died and Park House became vacant. The house was far too large for her mother on her own, so the Althorps took over the lease and Frances moved back into her old home.

In those early days, theirs was a particularly busy and happy life. Lord Althorp took over the running of his wife's farm quite close to Sandringham. He devoted much of his spare time to his many charities, including the local branch of the National Association of Boys Clubs, an association of which he is Chairman today. Their second daughter, Jane, was born in 1957 and despite a competent nanny and a full indoor staff of cook, housekeeper and butler, Lady Althorp took an active part in the running of the nursery and her house. They were considered the very pillars of Norfolk society and although Lord Althorp was no longer in the Queen's Household, they remained firm friends with all the members of the Royal Family. They dined at Sandringham when they were in residence or stayed at Balmoral in Scotland whenever Lord Althorp was asked to shoot. The son and heir, John, was born on 12 January 1960 but tragically died the same day. It was a terrible blow to both parents and Lady Althorp felt the loss especially deeply. Today, there is a sad little tombstone to the baby in Sandringham church beside that of his maternal grandfather, Lord Fermoy.

Naturally, the Althorps wanted another son and when their third daughter,

16. Lady Althorp holding her two-month-old baby, Diana, outside Park House on the Sandringham estate, Norfolk, in September 1961.

Diana, was born, they had not even considered any names in the advent of a girl. Still, she was a happy addition to a contented family and her parents doted on her. Her father remembers her, with transparent pride, as a 'delightful child, and as a baby she could have won any beauty competition'. She was certainly an even-tempered child, and was looked after in her early years by a young nanny from Kent, Judith Parnell. Although the youngest child, Diana was not spoilt but she did command most of her mother's and her nanny's attention. When she was three, however, her brother Charles was born and her own 'baby-days' were quickly at an end.

17. Sarah Spencer holding her baby sister, Diana, with her middle sister, Jane, at a garden party at Park House.

The next stage in Diana's life was to join her sisters in the schoolroom. The same Miss Allen, who had taught her mother, moved back into Park House to teach Sarah and Jane and some of their neighbours' children. One member of that class was Robert Fellowes, who is now married to Jane and is Assistant Private Secretary to the Queen. His father, Sir William Fellowes, retired as the Queen's land agent and was succeeded by Julian Loyd, whose daughter, Alexandra, joined Diana's class. The two have been firm friends ever since. Diana's early schooling was little different to her mother's except that Miss Allen was called 'Ally' and the schoolroom was moved from a room beside the front door to the butler's pantry, and redecorated with a bright wallpaper of leaves and balloons.

'Ally' was a Norfolk institution. She had spent all her life as a governess and she taught with a mixture of firmness and humour. Diana learned the three 'Rs' essential to country-house living—reading, writing, arithmetic—and also the fourth 'R', riding, which, however, was not on Ally's curriculum. Each child had

18. Aged three, Diana is with her mother at the wedding of her uncle, Lord Fermoy, in 1964.

an end-of-term report and Ally thought Diana a 'real trier' and a 'conscientious worker'. Later, she remembered her also as 'a relaxed child but somewhat serious' and a 'tidy soul'. History was one of Diana's favourite subjects—kings and queens, 'not battles'. Such an interest was to be expected in a girl whose neighbours were queens, princesses and princes, particularly her near-contemporary Andrew and his brother Edward who were seen at various times of the year.

The schoolroom was not the only place where Diana followed in the footsteps of her mother. She discovered the pleasures of the countryside that her mother had enjoyed as a child and she took the same walks and built houses in the same trees. Diana played identical games to those her mother had played and went to the same families and houses for childrens' parties. This common Norfolk background is still a strong bond between them today. Animals, too, played a major part in the lives of the Spencer children and they spent much of their time in the stables where they were kept. Sarah had a scruffy pony, Jane had rabbits and Diana favoured 'anything small enough to go in a cage', like hamsters, gerbils or guinea pigs. They vied for the privilege of looking after their father's shooting dogs, mostly springer spaniels.

50

The three daughters have very different characters and even in those early days, they were quite marked. Sarah, being the eldest, was by far the most extrovert and she immediately assumed the role of leader, while Jane was quiet and reserved and content to be dominated by her sister. Diana was somewhere between the two in temperament and her parents were pleased with the way she grew up as a thoughtful child. Her father remembers her as the one who would always put the log on the fire or shut the shutters on a cold winter's night.

The only friction in the family was the 'bad blood' between Lord Althorp and his father, Earl Spencer. They had not spoken to each other for years. Diana would occasionally be taken to visit her grandfather at their family seat of Althorp, but only by her mother. In the summer of 1967, a far greater family ruction upset the happy nursery life at Park House. Since the beginning of the year, the Althorps' marriage had been in difficulties and soon after Diana's sixth birthday they decided on a trial separation. When Sarah and Jane went back to their boarding school, Lady Althorp took the two younger children to a house she had taken in London. Diana went to a day school while Charles, just three, attended a kindergarten in the mornings. It was an amicable arrangement whereby Lord Althorp stayed with his wife and children when in London and Lady Althorp returned to Park House for the older girls' half-term and the holidays. During that first Christmas holiday, it was evident that their marriage had completely broken down and Lady Althorp later returned to London. Lord Althorp took Diana and Charles out of their respective London schools and enrolled them at a local school. Lady Althorp naturally wanted her children with her, and applied to the courts for their return to her care. When the case finally came up in June 1968, the judge gave custody to Lord Althorp, the fact that the children had spent most of their lives at Sandringham swaying the balance in his favour.

The inevitable scandal followed and Norfolk society quickly closed ranks to protect Lord Althorp and his children, being generous with offers of help and loud in their condemnation of Lady Althorp. Their help was not enough, however, to shield the children entirely from the publicity that followed the separation, the naming of their mother in the divorce of Peter Shand Kydd and his wife, Janet and, two years later, the acrimonious divorce of Lord and Lady Althorp. It was Diana's first taste of publicity which, although deeply upsetting at the time, was not as bad for her as for her older sisters.

Life continued at Park House without Lady Althorp. A series of *au pairs* were engaged but none stayed for long. Lord Althorp coped as best he could with the running of the house and the care of the children but he was lost without his wife. It was Lady Fermoy who stepped in. With great tact, she organised the children's lives and returned the equilibrium to the household. She gave them all the time she could spare from her busy Court schedule and was always there when she was needed most during holidays or to make important decisions.

The local school Lord Althorp had chosen for Diana was a day school, Silfield, in King's Lynn. Being the only private school in the area, it drew its fifty pupils

19. Diana at Park House during the summer of 1967 with her brother Charles on the swing.

from the town and the surrounding villages. The headmistress, Miss Lowe, still teaches in very much a 'traditional manner' in her school with its three classes, each one in a long wooden shed in the gardens of her house. Miss Lowe had taken Lord Althorp's side over the divorce and gave evidence in the proceedings for custody of the children.

Every weekday morning, wearing the school uniform of red and grey, Diana and Alexandra Loyd were driven into King's Lynn. Diana did well and enjoyed the school and, as a special prize for trying hard, Lord Althorp imported a camel from Dudley Zoo for Diana's seventh birthday. Her next birthday was memorable in another way because it was on the same day as the Investiture of the Prince of Wales at Caernarvon Castle on 1 July 1969. Diana remembers that holiday better, however, as the one when she fell off her pony and broke her arm. It was a bad break and took over two months to mend, as a result of which she lost her nerve with horses and has not ridden since.

The family rift was partially healed when Diana's mother married Peter Shand Kydd and they moved to a farm house outside Itchenor in West Sussex with his three children. Diana, and her brother and sisters, spent part of each holiday with them in Sussex or in their mother's London flat in Cadogan Place. Occasionally they went to their cousins, the Hughes-Wake-Walkers in Suffolk.

Although Diana could have stayed at Silfield School until she was eleven, it was decided that it would be better to send her to a boarding school. The obvious choice was another Norfolk school, Riddlesworth Hall, near Diss. The first day of the Michaelmas term 1969, Lord Althorp drove his nine-year-old daughter the forty miles to the school. He remembered it as 'a dreadful day, dreadful losing her' as he left his youngest daughter at the fine Georgian country house set in an open park. Along with Diana he unloaded a tuck box with her favourite treats of chocolate cake, ginger biscuits and Twiglets, a small travelling cage with her white-and-tan guinea-pig, Peanuts, and a trunk marked 'D. F. Spencer', filled with the result of a trip to Harrods, the school outfitter. The clothes' list seemed interminable with cherry sweaters, white shirts, grey pleated skirts for everyday wear, and cherry red dresses, known by the girls as 'prickles', for Sundays and special occasions.

To begin with, Diana suffered from homesickness but she had many Norfolk friends already at the school and in her 'term' and she soon settled down. Part of the success of Riddlesworth Hall was due to the kindly headmistress, Miss Elizabeth Ridesdale, known as 'Riddy'. She was an ideal person to take charge of Diana as she knew what to expect from the former pupils of Miss Allen and Silfield School and, in her twenty years as headmistress, she was experienced in dealing with girls from broken homes.

Undoubtedly made Riddlesworth Hall's most famous pupil by her marriage, Diana left her mark on the school in her own right. Their memory of her is recorded in the school magazine, written by Miss Ridesdale in August 1981 after the Royal Wedding:

One afternoon in 1970, a little girl came with her father to begin her school days at Riddlesworth Hall. This was the Honourable Diana Spencer. She must have felt nervous and even apprehensive tackling the unknown. However, very soon Diana settled in and became one of the family. She spent three-and-a-half years with us and made a warm place for herself in the school. The things that particularly stand out in my memories of her are her kindness to the smaller members of the community, her general helpfulness, her love of animals and her excellence at swimming and indeed her considerable prowess in general physical activities. Having taken her Common Entrance she then passed onto West Heath.

She was awarded a cup called 'Pets Corner' in recognition for her work in the 'shanty town of hutches in a grove known as the 'ghost walk' opposite the front door'. Her general helpfulness was also rewarded with another cup. The juniors at the school remembered her, not only for her kindness, but as a high-spirited girl.

Although Diana passed her Common Entrance Examination 'quite well' she was no academic and her forte, like her mother, was on the games field. Her success at swimming was due not only to the good grounding she received at Riddlesworth Hall but also to the new heated swimming pool Lord Spencer had installed at Park House, which she used during the holidays. Her tennis improved as a result of the coaching she received from a Mrs Landsdowne.

In the summer of 1973, Diana went to visit her mother and stepfather, Peter Shand Kydd, at the farm they had just bought on the Isle of Seil on the west coast of Scotland. It was an important time for Diana. She was then twelve and more able to appreciate those headstrong and forceful qualities in her mother. Although brought up largely by her father and Lady Fermoy in Norfolk, she now grew closer to her mother and was to be influenced by her strength of character. She enjoyed, too, the life on the Shand Kydds' farm, Ardencaple. When not helping with the sheep and cattle, Diana with her sisters, brother, step-relations or any friend who happened to be staying, would explore the island or go across Telford's 'Bridge over the Atlantic' to the mainland and walk over the hills. There were no idle moments. There were lobster pots to be baited, put down and collected, or Diana would go in her stepfather's sailing boat trolling for mackerel. She often went swimming, although there were few other takers for the cold Atlantic waters. Their life was simple in the whitewashed farm house. Entertainment was of their own making, and occasionally they visited the cinema in Oban. Not for them the smart Highland Balls through the summer, but rather the fun gatherings in the Oban Town Hall. Diana loved it all and developed in the process a permanent taste for the ways and countryside of Scotland.

Great care had been taken in choosing Diana's final school. She needed a place that would not push her limited academic ability, but would foster her love of music and games and develop her sense of responsibility and her caring nature. Eventually her parents decided on West Heath, a girls' public school near Sevenoaks in Kent. It was an ideal choice and Diana arrived at the school for the

20. Diana at Itchenor, West Sussex, during the part of the holidays of 1970 that she spent with her mother and step-father.

21. Diana with the prize-winning guinea-pig, Peanuts, at the Sandringham Show 1972.

Michaelmas term 1973, aged twelve, with her friend from Norfolk and Riddlesworth Hall, Caroline Harboard Hammond.

The Australian headmistress, Miss Ruth Rudge, believed in treating each of her 130 pupils as an individual and she upheld to the full the West Heath traditions of developing 'their own minds and tastes and to help them realise their own duties as citizens'. The school catered equally for academically-inclined girls and for those with just common sense, so the pupils tended to be drawn from rather more interesting or unusual backgrounds than in other girls' schools. Also, they were taken on their particular merit rather than on their parents' ability to pay the school fees.

Like Riddlesworth Hall, West Heath was a Georgian house and retained that same country-house atmosphere. The gardens were exceptional. On one side of the sweeping lawns was a Japanese water garden with bamboo thickets and on the other, the American garden was, according to a former pupil, 'ravishingly lovely in June when the herbaceous borders were all in flower and the four banks of azaleas and rhododendrons were out'.

As part of the policy of promoting the individuality of the girls, there was no West Heath school uniform but the girls were expected to wear a navy skirt, a shirt and tie for lessons. On Sundays, like the rest of the girls, Diana could wear what she liked—a sharp contrast in church to the smartly uniformed girls from the many other girls' schools present.

West Heath was screened into six forms, each one with eight grades. The three lower forms were Cedar, Poplar and Cypress and the three upper were Beech, Elm and Oak—Oak being the equivalent to a sixth form. Diana entered at the bottom, Cedar, but advanced through her grades rapidly, not so much because of her prowess at lessons, which attracted comment like 'normal' or 'average', quite often 'tried hard', but rather because of her 'duty as a citizen'. Throughout her school career, Diana excelled at that intrinsic West Heath idea of service to the community.

Every week, Diana would visit an old lady in Sevenoaks. She would sit and talk to her, taking a genuine interest in her welfare, and would also help in practical ways like doing some of her housework or the week's shopping. On another afternoon in the week she would visit a centre for handicapped children. The children loved her and she took enormous pleasure in reading or playing games with them. It was then that she realised that she had a natural talent with children—'a positive pied piper with children', her mother said later—and that she wanted to work with them. She was also popular with the staff as she was not above doing the most menial of tasks with willingness and a smile. At the end of her time at West Heath, she was given a 'special award for service'. It was a discretionary award and only presented to outstanding pupils. Miss Rudge later confirmed that she was a worthy recipient, and that 'Diana was genuinely surprised to have won it'.

Music was another essential part of a West Heath education. There were two school choirs and outings to concerts in London were a regular feature every term. Diana continued with her piano lessons but soon abandoned them in favour of ballet and tap-dancing. Later, she admitted that she was 'obsessed with ballet and I also love tap-dancing. I always wanted to be a ballet dancer and started taking lessons when I was three-and-a-half. But I just grew too tall.' Indeed, she is 5 ft 10 in, the same height as her mother.

Like her mother, too, Diana shone most on the games field. She became captain of hockey but swimming was still her best sport. She was captain of the swimming and diving team and won every aquatic cup in the school. In the year of her captaincy, there were no equals in that sport among the many girls' schools around West Heath.

When Diana was almost fourteen, another event dramatically changed her life. In June 1975, her grandfather, the 7th Earl Spencer, died. Her father now became the eighth Earl and she, as his daughter, was the Lady Diana Spencer, her sisters Lady Sarah and Lady Jane, and her brother Charles became Viscount Althorp. With the title her father took over Althorp and the estate not far from Northampton. Despite its size and fabulous collection of art, books and furniture—of its kind, as good as in any royal Palace—Althorp is not a museum. Lord Spencer was determined that it should be a home for his children and went to great lengths to make it so. For his family he installed an outdoor heated swimming pool and a tennis court and he redecorated bedrooms in the nursery wing for Diana and Charles. Sarah, then aged twenty, and Jane, eighteen, who were both living in London, also had their own rooms at Althorp.

The holidays at Althorp were little different to Park House. The Earl Spencer remembers her, soon after they moved, playing 'bears in the park' in the long picture gallery lined with portraits of her ancestors, and 'flying down the front stairs on a tea-tray'. Later, Diana and her brother were to be seen driving round the estate in a sky-blue beach buggy. They were happy times and Diana often invited her Norfolk and school friends to stay.

Just as the Spencer family were settling into their new home and the shared holidays between the parents became an amicable matter of course, a drastic event occurred that was to cause another scandal and invite further publicity. After the Althorps' divorce, Lord Spencer made no secret of the fact that he needed to find a mother 'for all those children'. He was to remain on his own for eight years until the arrival of the Countess of Dartmouth. Earl Spencer had been in the same house at Eton as the Earl of Dartmouth and subsequently he had met the Countess of Dartmouth, the daughter of Barbara Cartland, the prolific romantic novelist. A forceful campaigner for cleanliness, both moral and physical, the Countess of Dartmouth was a Westminster City Councillor and was later elected onto the Greater London Council. Their friendship grew to a point where she left her husband and moved into Althorp with Lord Spencer. Diana was fifteen at the time and quite old enough to understand what was happening. Her sisters and staff were vociferous in their resentment of Lady Dartmouth, her presence at Althorp and the sweeping changes she made to the house and estate so soon after the old Lord Spencer had died.

Once again, Diana was forced to witness her family laid open to public scrutiny in the press and comment amongst the girls at her school when Lord Dartmouth sued for divorce on the grounds of the irrevocable breakdown of his marriage. Lady Dartmouth was now free to marry Lord Spencer which she did at a London Registry Office in July 1976. Their wedding, too, was much publicised because his children were absent, which was not surprising as they were only told after the event. Nevertheless, Diana coped well with the publicity and her headmistress, Miss Rudge, helped her through the ordeal with understanding and sympathy.

Towards the end of Diana's last term at West Heath, November 1977, Miss Rudge allowed her home for a very special weekend. The Earl and Countess Spencer had invited Sarah's friend, the Prince of Wales, to stay for the weekend at Althorp and to shoot on the Saturday. Diana was driven up on that morning and joined the guns on the last drive before lunch. It was while walking back for lunch, across a ploughed field, that Sarah introduced the Prince of Wales to her sister. They walked on together and Prince Charles, during their press interview on the afternoon of their engagement, recalled the scene, remembering her as 'a splendid sixteen-year-old, full of fun'.

That night, when the house party met in the Marlborough Room, Lord Spencer was immensely proud of Diana. He was much impressed by her appearance and noticed the apparent ease with which she talked to the rest of the party, including the Prince of Wales and the neighbours who had been asked to dinner. It was then that he realised that his daughter had outgrown the nursery and her school and that her childhood was truly over.

The success of the Princess of Wales is partly due to the influence of her mother and partly to the close bond with her sisters. It was this closeness that helped them all cope with the respective trials and tribulations of their early lives. They were all deeply affected by the bitterness of their parents' divorce and there were times when their lives were very strained.

Jane's answer to the problem was to marry young, and happily. She now has a three-year-old daughter, Laura, to whom the Princess of Wales is a devoted aunt. The path to happiness was not as direct and simple for her sister Sarah, the eldest of the three. She suffered from anorexia nervosa, a complaint common amongst the children of divorced parents. She had known Prince Charles for much of her life, and for a few months accompanied him at various social functions. The press escalated their easy, uncomplicated friendship into marital proportions and eventually Sarah felt she was forced to make her position known: 'I am not in love with him . . . and I wouldn't marry anyone I didn't love, whether it was the dustman or the King of England. If he asked me, I would turn him down.' The press, who had dogged her every move, dropped her, and subsequently Sarah did exactly what she said she would do and married a farmer, Neil McCorquodale, for love and love alone.

This left Diana, a teenager and still at school, who, at the time her sister's name was linked with that of Prince Charles, was already, according to the

22. Lady Diana Spencer with her mother, the Hon. Mrs Shand Kydd, at the wedding of Lady Sarah Spencer at Althorp, Northamptonshire in May 1980.

headmistress of her finishing school at Chateau d'Oex, in love with him herself. If that is so, it must have been very difficult for her, being so close to both parties, to be forced to wait silently for the outcome. Undoubtedly, early on in their relationship, Sarah confided to her younger sister that, as far as she was concerned, there was no possibility of marriage, but for Diana, as in the oldest and best fairy tales, things had to be bad before they became right. In the televised interview on the day of her engagement, she was asked if it was hard to decide whether Prince Charles was the right man for her. Without a moment's hesitation, she replied: 'it wasn't a difficult decision in the end. It was what I wanted—it's what I want.'

Now that all three sisters have what they want in life, they remain as close as ever. Jane and Sarah continue to support Diana, appearing with her on the occasional public function and, of all the family, it was Sarah who showed the most delight at her sister's engagement. She gave her much valuable support and advice, both before and after that engagement, and showed concern that Diana was being asked to do too much, too early—for example, condemning the ball at Buckingham Palace only two days before the wedding.

Few can doubt how magnificently the Princess of Wales has survived the anxieties of her life, and all with a grace and maturity far beyond her years. Few can also have failed to have been moved by the transformation in St Paul's Cathedral on the day of her wedding from a girl to a princess. Diana commented during her engagement that her mother should be proud to have 'married off' three daughters at such a young age. That those three daughters should have remained so close and be of such support to each other, and that one of them is now Princess of Wales, is something of which both Mrs Shand Kydd and Lord Spencer are indeed proud.

PART TWO

The Royal Families

1

Queen Victoria and her Children

The death in childbirth in 1817 of Princess Charlotte, George III's only legitimate grandchild and daughter of the Prince Regent, precipitated the scramble of his three bachelor sons to marry and produce an heir in order to continue the Hanoverian line. William, Duke of Clarence (later to become 'the Sailor King', William IV) and Edward, Duke of Kent, both abandoned their long-standing mistresses and, with their brother Adolphus, Duke of Cambridge, all married within two months of each other in 1818.

Edward married Victoire, widow of the Prince of Leiningen and went to live with her in her house in that small German principality. At thirty-one, she was plump, pretty, and the sister of Prince Leopold of Saxe-Coburg-Saalfeld, the widower of Princess Charlotte. Within six weeks, Victoire was pregnant and she and Edward returned to his apartments at Kensington Palace so that a possible heir to the throne would be born in England. Their daughter was born on 24 May 1819. She was a healthy child, later described by Baron Stockmar as 'a pretty little Princess, as plump as a partridge'. Both the Duke, who was present at the birth, and the Duchess were thrilled with their child. Outside the immediate family, however, the news of the birth of the future Queen Victoria, monarch of the largest and most powerful empire the world has ever seen, was greeted with scant enthusiasm and in some quarters, decided hostility. The clue to this animosity lay with her parents, for of all George III's fifteen children, the Duke of Kent was the most unpopular, notorious as a martinet and a profligate. The Prince Regent disliked the Duchess intensely, simply because she was the sister of Prince Leopold, his widowed son-in-law, whom he also loathed.

At an acrimonious service in Kensington Palace, the baby was christened Alexandrina Victoria. In her early years, she was known as 'Drina', although she adopted her second name, Victoria, on her accession as Queen.

Despite the increase in his allowance when he married, the Duke of Kent was still hopelessly in debt. In order to economise, and to escape the hostility of his brothers, he moved after Christmas, 1819, to Woolbrook Cottage, a small, damp house in pretty surroundings near Sidmouth on the south coast of Devon. It was an abnormally harsh winter but although her parents suffered the boredom and chill of the place, the seven-month-old Victoria thrived—'too healthy I fear', her father wrote, 'in the opinion of some members of my family.' Their stay, however, was soon over. The Duke went out to look at his horses with his equerry, Captain John Conroy, and caught a heavy cold. The cold worsened to pneumonia and he died on 23 January. Fortunately for the Duchess, her brother was at hand to take complete charge. Prince Leopold arranged for her, Victoria and the two children of her first marriage, Charles and Feodora, to return to Kensington Palace, and made them a gift of £3,000 a year out of the £50,000 annual allowance he still received from his marriage to Princess Charlotte. From her husband, whom she adored, she inherited nothing but his debts and the services of John Conroy, to act as the Comptroller of her Household, such as it was.

As a baby at Kensington Palace, Victoria appears to have been a forward and remarkably healthy child. According to an anonymous account at that time, she was

> a beautiful child, bearing a very strong resemblance to her father, and indeed the royal family generally. Though small and delicately formed, she was very fat, and might be called a remarkably fine child for her age; her eyes were large and blue; her complexion extremely fair, with a rosy colour expressive of high health, and her curled lips continually parted, shewing her four pretty white teeth. She was forward in her speech; very lively, and appeared of a gentle, happy temper; occasionally a sweet and merry smile animated her intelligent countenance.

Nearly fifty years later, Queen Victoria wrote of her childhood: 'My earliest recollections [aged nearly two] are connected with Kensington Palace. I can recall crawling on a yellow carpet spread out for that purpose—and being told that if I cried and was naughty my Uncle [the Duke of] Sussex would hear me and punish me ... for which reason I always screamed when I saw him!' She remembered that she 'used to ride a donkey given to me by the Duke of York who was very kind to me ... and he had Punch and Judy for me in the garden.' She recalled that 'the King [George IV] had been on bad terms with my poor father when he died, and then hardly took any notice of a poor widow and little girl ... When we arrived at Royal Lodge, the King took me by the hand, saying, "Give me your little paw".'

The young Victoria, by her own admission, was 'much indulged by everyone ... old Baroness de Spaeth, the devoted Lady of my Mother, my nurse, Mrs Brock [affectionately known by her as 'Boppy'], dear old Mrs Louis [Princess Charlotte's dresser]—*all* worshipped the poor little fatherless child.' She was an affectionate little girl who returned the love of not only the nursery staff but also of her mother and of her step-sister Feodora, twelve years her senior.

Victoria's early years were eventful. In the summer months the family went to Ramsgate, travelling by paddle-steamer which 'made Mama very unwell'. There, 'Her Royal Highness was occasionally permitted to play with the children of the gentry, whom she met on the beach', but, being an independent child, she was content to make sand-castles and paddle on her own, under the constant supervision of her nurse. Both she and Feodora loved staying at Claremont in Surrey with their Uncle Leopold—'the brightest epoch of my rather melancholy childhood'—and both children cried when they had to return to Kensington.

It was the Duke of Kent's wish that when Victoria reached the age of five, her nurse, Mrs Brock, should be replaced by Louise Lehzen, a formidable woman who had been brought over from Hanover to act as governess to Feodora. Lehzen, as she was invariably known, was 'a clever, agreeable woman' of thirty-five. She had been in Sidmouth when the Duke died and thus had known Victoria since babyhood. From an early age, Victoria had had that terrible Hanoverian temper when reprimanded or denied anything. She would shout and scream, stamping her feet in a fury. Once, she even threw a pair of scissors at Lehzen. With Lehzen's sympathetic but firm handling, Victoria managed to master her temper. In her reminiscences, Queen Victoria wrote of Lehzen: 'She never for the 13 years she was governess to Pss Victoria, once left her . . . The Princess was her only object and her only thought. She was very strict and the Pss had great respect and even awe of her, but with that the greatest affection.'

Life at Kensington Palace for the young Princess was simple. Victoria never had a room of her own and up to the morning when she became Queen, she slept in her mother's bedroom. The routine of the day varied little. 'Breakfast was at half-past eight, luncheon at half-past one, dinner at seven—to which I [Victoria] generally came (when there was no large dinner party)—eating my bread and milk out of a silver basin. Tea was only allowed as a great treat in later years.' It was a dull existence with little to enliven it, and apart from those brief moments on the sands at Ramsgate when she played with other children, Victoria's childhood was spent almost exclusively dominated by adult women or amusing herself. She played with her large collection of dolls, 132 of them, a substitute for the playmates her mother denied her. She adored her mother's King Charles spaniel, 'dear Dashy', and the parakeet kept in the nursery and later, a Shetland pony called Rosa.

The Duchess of Kent, who was at first a sympathetic and loving mother, was soon to alter. The change came through the influence of John Conroy, her Comptroller, an Irishman with an easy charm and great ambition, who could see that when Victoria became queen his aspiration to great power, through his hold over her mother, would be fulfilled. He instituted what was to become known as the 'Kensington System' whereby Victoria was to become totally dependent on her mother and her mother on him. To insure that Victoria was moulded into the person they wanted, they removed all opposition to their plan. To this end, the Baroness de Spaeth was dismissed after twenty-five years of devoted service. Conroy then contrived to inflame the long-standing antagonism between the Duchess and her daughter and the Court. He even sent his own daughter to play with Victoria once a week, but Victoria disliked her as much as her father. The more her mother needed Conroy, the closer Victoria moved to Lehzen. To observers outside Kensington Palace, Victoria seemed a happy child but, in reality, she was lonely, living in an atmosphere of intrigue and unhappiness, a life totally ordered by Conroy.

It was not until 1827, when Victoria was eight years old, that her formal education began. Around the age of five, she had been taught 'her letters', but Victoria was 'not fond of learning as a little child'. Under a clergyman called George Davys, she worked to a set timetable. The accent of the lessons was on modern languages, taught by visiting tutors, and on music, drawing and dancing. She learnt Latin, with difficulty, and arithmetic 'for which she had a particular talent', while at geography and history she 'was better informed than most young persons of the same age'. She worked well and, apart from reports of inattention—'absence of mind'—her tutors and mother were satisfied with her progress, as were the panel of Bishops who set her examinations in March, 1830.

For some unexplained reason, the Duchess of Kent did not tell her daughter that it was probable that she would be queen and hoped that she 'would come to the knowledge by accident in pursuing her education'. By the early part of 1830, George IV was dying, predeceased by his childless brother, Frederick, Duke of York. His heir, William, Duke of Clarence, was also heirless, his two daughters having died at birth and three months. This made Victoria heir presumptive. When the eleven-year-old Victoria eventually found out how close she was to the throne (Lehzen had slipped a chronological table into her history book), she cried bitterly. But she soon realised what was expected of her and, according to Lehzen, replied, 'I see I am nearer to the throne than I thought. Now, there is much splendour, but there is more responsibility! . . . I will be good.'

George IV died in June 1830 and the new king, William IV and his wife Adelaide, were fond of their niece, and, as heir presumptive, a renewed interest was taken in the eleven-year-old Victoria. Reports of her appearance and character varied; Charles Greville, the celebrated diarist, described her as 'a short vulgar-looking child', while the Tory, Lady Wharncliffe, was

> delighted with our little future Queen. She is very much grown though short for her age, has a nice countenance and distingué figure, tho' not very good; and her manner is the most perfect mixture of childishness and civility I ever saw . . . She is really very accomplished by taste, being very fond of both music and drawing, but fondest of all of her dolls. In short I look to her to save us from Democracy, for it is impossible she should not be popular when she is older and more seen.

The older Victoria became, the more she was 'seen'. Her mother, to the intense annoyance of the King, showed her daughter off in a series of tours around England and Wales. These 'royal progresses' were a great success and Victoria was fêted and cheered wherever she went. On one such tour to the Midlands, Yorkshire and East Anglia, in the autumn of 1835, she complained of a severe headache, nausea and pains in her back. After the tour, she was taken to Ramsgate to recuperate but she collapsed and was 'very ill'. Conroy dismissed it as 'a mere disposition', Dr Clark 'a bilious fever', but it is now thought that she had tonsilitis. When Victoria recovered, she returned to Kensington Palace and the same discordant rule of the dreaded Conroy and the ravings and intrigues of her mother. Lessons with Davys began again, and she began to study more advanced subjects like anatomy, English constitutional history and French and English classics. Three times a week, Lehzen took her for long walks on Hampstead Heath as prescribed by her doctor. She was bored and 'longed sadly for some gaiety'. She enjoyed the plays or operas she saw on her fortnightly visits. She loved what she described as 'mirth'—amusing conversation, dancing and music which her mother, and Conroy, tried to deny her.

In the spring of 1836, when Victoria was just seventeen, Leopold, now King of the Belgians, sent his two nephews to England to stay at Kensington Palace. Since the day of his birth, Leopold had decided that the younger brother, Albert of Saxe-Coburg, would marry his niece. After their first meeting, Victoria found her cousins 'very amiable, very kind and good, and extremely merry, just as young people ought to be . . . and Albert is extremely good-looking.' Victoria wrote to her uncle and pronounced that she would be happy to marry him when the time came.

Conroy's plans were thwarted, however, when Victoria reached the age of eighteen before the old King died. There could be no Regency and Conroy's lifelong ambition was finished. He knew that Victoria detested him for making her childhood a misery and alienating her mother and her father's family from her. Within a month of her eighteenth birthday, William IV died. On 20 June, 1837 Victoria was woken at dawn to meet the Archbishop of Canterbury and the Lord Chancellor, Lord Conyngham, who told her that, 'the King was no more, and had expired at 12 minutes past 2 this morning and consequently that *I* am *Queen.*'

The young Queen Victoria lost no time in catching up on the excitement and 'mirth' that was lacking in her childhood. Her new life was bright and energetic; she indulged herself with an endless round of dancing and banquets, operas and the theatres. Her Uncle Leopold made her invite her cousins, Ernest and Albert of Saxe-Coburg, for a short holiday in the autumn of 1839, and when the party arrived at Windsor, rather dishevelled from a bad Channel crossing, she saw Albert from the top of the stairs. Of that first sight, after an absence of three years, she later wrote: 'It was with some emotion that I beheld Albert—who is *beautiful.*' The Queen was in love and that love was reciprocated. Three months later, on 10 February 1840, they were married.

The life of Queen Victoria's Court continued at the same hectic pace after her marriage and when she found that she was pregnant at the beginning of May, she was far from excited. But Albert was delighted and he, who at twenty had never even held a baby, drew up a treatise on how their child, undoubtedly a boy, should be brought up and educated as a future monarch. It was a laboured work, pompous and unreal, which has since made Albert appear an insensitive disciplinarian. Their confidant, Baron Stockmar, dismissed it, commenting that if it were followed to the letter the child 'would die of brain fever'. However, what Stockmar did advise was that, in view of the parents' youth, they should have an experienced and intelligent woman to take charge of their nursery and he encouraged them to appoint a Mrs Southey, the widow of a friend of his, who, as it later turned out, was an unsatisfactory choice.

The first of Queen Victoria and Albert's nine children was born a fortnight early on 22 November 1840. Victoria Adelaide Mary Louise, the Princess Royal, was 'a perfect little child . . . but alas a girl and not a boy as we had so hoped and wished for'. Albert, however, was to 'make a capital nurse, which I do not', the Queen wrote as she handed her baby over to a wet-nurse. 'Pussy', as her father called the baby, was sickly and, when weaned, began to lose weight. The real trouble lay with the ineffectual nursery staff, with the inadequate Mrs Southey, and with the interference of Lahzen, the Queen's old governess, now raised to the rank of Baroness and Lady Companion. With Stockmar's backing, Albert sent them all away and engaged the 'sensible and motherly Mrs Sly' as nurse and appointed Lady Lyttleton as 'Lady Superintendent'. Sarah Lyttleton was a widow of fifty with five children of her own and before her marriage she was a Spencer—an ancestress of the present Princess of Wales. For eight years she was to care for the royal children and a large part of the success of their upbringing can be attributed to her régime. She was conscientious and loved her charges, reporting to their mother daily on their health, mental state and general progress. Food in the nursery was plain, sparse and simple—fare that newly-engaged nursery-maids could not believe. 'We eat better at home', one remarked. In order to combat germs, fresh air, open windows and small fires were the norm, as well as cold baths for them all every morning. Clothes, too, were plain and were handed on to the next brother or sister. It was indeed an austere nursery existence.

Twelve days before Vicky's first birthday, 9 November 1841, the son and heir to the Queen and Albert was born. He was christened Albert Edward and created Prince of Wales soon after but, to his family, he was always known as 'Bertie'. He was a chubby child, pale with grey-blue eyes and soft brown hair, a direct contrast to his sister with her rosy complexion, deep-blue eyes and a head of fair curls. The contrast did not end there. Where Vicky was bright and quick, learning to speak early, Bertie was dull and somewhat backward in walking and talking. However, his parents and the nursery staff were besotted with the boy and, throughout his childhood, he was never short of affection and constant attention. Only Vicky, out of jealousy, initially failed to warm to him. His slowness to speak was later found to be caused by a mild stutter and this inability to make himself properly understood partially contributed to his childhood tantrums. As he grew older, these violent rages increased, and his parents and nurses feared for his, and, later, the other childrens' safety. In a frightening display of anger, he would shout and scream, bite and lash out with any handy weapon. Mrs Sly, the nurse, frightened of provoking such a rage, indulged him with whatever he wanted, which only added to the problem. Vicky, too, was initially somewhat of a problem with her volatile temper but her outbursts were invariably caused by the frustration of being so advanced for her age. However, she soon learned that charm, rather than temper, ensured that she had her own way.

A second daughter, Alice Maud Mary, was born on 25 April 1843. Alice was a plump, jolly, spirited child, and the Queen and Albert were more relaxed in her upbringing. By comparison with other Victorian households, and contrary to popular belief, the royal nursery was remarkably liberal. Punishments meted out by Albert or by Lady Lyttleton, 'Ladle' as she became known, were seldom harsh. She wrote, 'I own I am against punishments, they wear out so soon and one is never sure they are fully understood by the child as belonging to the naughtiness.' Instead, censure took the form of the loss of a treat, like a favoured walk or a ride with their parents, or being sent to bed early without dinner, all of which had greater effect than 'a sound whipping'.

The Queen and Albert had complete faith in Lady Lyttleton so that, knowing that everything in the nursery was well, they could enjoy their children to the full. They never tried to interfere with their upbringing or give orders, except to make absolutely certain that none of their children grew up too proud of their birth and position. In the same vein, rudeness to servants was never tolerated. The Queen insisted that, 'the greatest maxim of all is that the children should be brought up as simply and in as domestic way as possible. They should be as much as possible with their parents and learn to place the greatest confidence in them in all things.'

On 6 August 1844, another royal baby, Alfred Ernest Albert, was born. Bright and cheerful, even-tempered and independent, gregarious, as well as being totally self-sufficient, everything, in fact, that his elder brother lacked were among the attributes of this model son. Although his parents did not love their other children any the less, 'Affie', as he was called in the family, was their favourite. These eldest four children, born within four years of each other, teamed up with one another, the two boys and the two girls together. Despite the marked contrast in their characters, Affie greatly admired his elder brother, just as Alice was protected by her elder sister, Vicky, and became her boon companion. But the older they became, the more Bertie was isolated by his terrible temper, and his poor showing with his brother and sisters only heightened his sense of inferiority. Even Alice, two years his junior, was taller than him. He was easily bored and had little concentration, but there were occasional moments of charm and endearment that gave his parents hope that he was improving.

Vicky, bright and advanced for her age, started her education early and a clergyman's daughter, Sarah Hildyard, nicknamed 'Tilla', was engaged to teach her before she was five years old. She was a great success and Vicky responded well to her sensible approach to teaching. When Bertie started to 'learn his letters' with Lady Lyttleton, something his sisters enjoyed, he rarely co-operated, hiding under the table and upsetting the others.

For the first years of their marriage, the Queen and Albert went to their seaside home at Brighton—the young parents believing in 'health-giving sea bathes'.

The Pavilion, too public and unsuitable for children, was sold and they went instead to Osborne House on the Isle of Wight. They bought Balmoral, near Aberdeen in Scotland, soon after and, as soon as these places were habitable, the children spent their holidays there. Another excitement from Osborne was to go on the new royal yacht, *Victoria and Albert*, or the smaller steam yacht, *Fairy*. Parents and children, particularly Affie with his mechanical and nautical bents, enjoyed the trips enormously. On holiday and away from affairs of state, the Queen and Albert had more time to devote to their children. They would all go off on picnics and sketching trips or Albert would take the boys stalking or fishing. They all loved dancing, particularly Highland dancing, and once a year the children were allowed to stay up for the 'ghillies' ball'.

The 'second quartet' of children began with the birth of Helena on 25 May 1846. From a 'blue baby', the result of a difficult birth, she was to grow into one of the most rumbustious of all the Queen's children. Known affectionately as 'Lenchen', she had none of the 'social graces' of her sisters, but that did not worry her as she preferred her horses and outdoor life to delicate embroidery, drawing or music. She was followed two years later on 18 March 1848, by the sixth child, Louise Caroline Alberta. Queen Victoria had always maintained that

23. Mrs Thurston, the nanny, holding the baby Princess Louise with (left to right) Albert Edward (Prince of Wales and later Edward VII), Princesses Helena and Victoria, their brother, Prince Alfred, and Princess Alice is on the ground (1848).

'an ugly baby is a very nasty object—and the prettiest is frightful when undressed—till about four months; in short, as long as they have their big body and little limbs and that terrible froglike action.' She could not have applied that description to her latest daughter for, according to Lady Augusta Bruce, she was 'that delicious baby Louise' with looks that she kept all her life. Even as a young child, her temperament was mercurial, although her parents simply put any defect in her character down to the artistic side of her nature. From the age of three she excelled at drawing and painting. Her mother, no mean artist herself, encouraged her and had Louise not been the Princess she was, she could have gone on to make a name for herself in the world of art.

After another gap of two years, the next baby arrived on 1 May 1850. If, in Queen Victoria's eyes, Affie was a model child, Arthur William Patrick Albert was a paragon. He seemed to embrace every good quality of all his brothers and sisters but none of the bad. As his birthday coincided with that of the popular Duke of Wellington, he was not only given his name but had him as a godfather. Consequently, from the day of his birth, he was destined for the army and his childhood announcement, 'Arta is going to be a soldier', was taken as a matter of course. Christmas and birthday presents had a military flavour, as did his games and reading. Albert, who called him 'Colonel Mention', built him a fort at Osborne and encouraged his passion for drawing up maps and planning battles. As he grew up, however, he drew apart from his brothers, who were much older while his sisters closer to his own age were simply not interested in his martial pursuits. Nor was his brother, Leopold, three years his junior.

Leopold George Duncan Albert was born on 7 April 1853 with the aid of 'blessed chloroform'. Despite this novel start to his life and the beneficial effect of the drug on his mother, 'little Leo' was a sickly baby. Later, when he began to walk and crash about the nursery, it was noticed that these minor knocks came out in angry bruises and 'Little Leo' was diagnosed as a haemophiliac. Throughout his childhood therefore, he was condemned to complete inactivity for fear of hurting himself and starting the internal bleeding that might kill him. However, he turned his sedentary life to his best advantage and learned to read young. With an avid thirst for knowledge, he showed all the intelligence of his sister Vicky at the same age. Albert took a particular interest in the boy, fostering his interest in art, carrying him round their various palaces, explaining each picture or piece of sculpture to him. Later, he taught him to paint. Leo showed a strong talent for music and made great progress with Mrs Anderson, who had taught all the children with varying degrees of success. He also enjoyed singing, particularly duets with his father. When well enough, Leo was allowed to ride and go for walks, or to collect geological specimens, as his father had done at the same age.

By the time Leopold was born, his eldest sister was nearly thirteen and Bertie almost twelve. Vicky continued in her quest for knowledge and her father took particular delight in teaching her himself, preparing her for her life ahead and fostering her interest in such subjects as philosophy, politics and history. It was he who stimulated her to read the best English, French and German literature. The other children, in turn, were taught by their parents, Albert taking them in the more advanced subjects, while the Queen took special pride and care in starting them in their religious lessons which, she believed, 'is best given to a child day by day at its mother's knee'.

The main problem for the Queen and Albert in those early years was Bertie and his education. They consulted Baron Stockmar who advised that, as heir to the throne, he should be educated in England and that the curriculum should be as open and varied as possible. Albert agreed that to cram him would defeat its own end. So he set out his timetable with considerable care, following a difficult lesson, like mathematics or English, with one less demanding, like drawing or music. After Bertie's inauspicious start to his education with Lady Lyttleton, he moved on to join his sisters in Sarah Hildyard's school room at the age of seven. When there was no improvement in Bertie's learning, a tutor, Henry Birch, was engaged to teach him although he continued with some of his lessons with his sisters. The new tutor was an excellent choice, young, intelligent and enthusiastic about his difficult task. He agreed with Albert on his gentle approach to the education of the heir to the throne, but he soon became

24. Queen Victoria driving herself with her older children (left to right), Princess Victoria and Alice with the Prince of Wales, 10 February 1857.

dispirited with the total lack of co-operation and general disinterest of his pupil. Any attempt to censure Bertie was met with another rage. Birch thought that healthy competition might stimulate his pupil and Affie joined him for lessons. The experiment worked initially and Bertie improved slightly. But Affie, much in awe of his elder brother, began to emulate him and the tutor soon had two unruly boys instead of just one. After two exhausting years, Henry Birch resigned, ostensibly to begin his career in the Church which he had delayed at the Queen's request. Bertie's parents were bitterly disappointed, the Queen believing that he was too similar to her where learning was concerned. As she later confided to Vicky, 'He is my caricature, that is my misfortune and in a man this is much worse'.

Birch was replaced by another tutor, Frederick Gibbs, a young Cambridge fellow and barrister. Contrary to general belief, Gibbs was a mild and sensitive man. History has branded him as the tyrant of the Prince of Wales's childhood but as his diaries too clearly show, it was he who was victimised by his pupil. Entries such as 'He [Bertie] struck me with a large stick in a passion' or 'he became violently angry because I wanted some Latin done; he flung things about, made grimaces, called me names and could not do anything for a long time' were common. Affie shared Bertie's lessons, and, despite the bullying from his elder brother, he remained loyal to him and emulated his behaviour. For his own good, the boys were separated in the schoolroom and Affie once more became a willing and interested pupil, to the delight of his parents.

Like Henry Birch, Gibbs, too, failed to educate Bertie and he was replaced by General Bruce, husband of one of the Queen's ladies-in-waiting. Albert also tried to teach his son, but, although spared the rudery, met with the same inattention. He kept his patience, although he could see that, when Bertie wanted, he was brighter than he usually showed himself to be.

When the Queen and Albert's last child was born, they had been married for seventeen years and their eldest daughter, Vicky, was engaged to Prince Frederick William of Prussia. Beatrice May Victoria Feodore was born 14 April 1857. She was an easy child and responded to the affection of her parents, brothers and sisters. As she grew up in the privileged state of the youngest of the family, 'Baby', as she was known for far too long, was indulged by them all. Her happy state did not last long, for at the age of four, her father died of typhoid fever on 14 December 1861.

With Albert's death, the children not only lost their beloved father, but also the happy, gentle mother they had known up to then. The Queen 'was overwhelmed with grief'. She was forty-two, and for the rest of her life she mourned 'her beloved Albert', wearing her black widow's weeds with a white lace cap which Beatrice called her 'sad cap'. They were sad days, too, for the Queen could not tolerate any form of amusement or gaiety. The effect on the older children was less harsh than on the younger. Vicky was already married and Bertie was up at Cambridge. Alice, who coped with her mother after Albert's death, soon left home to marry and Affie was happy in the Navy. To Helena the

25. Princess Beatrice, the youngest of Queen Victoria's children, in her cradle, aged just three weeks, 1857.

26. Princess Beatrice taking her first ride on her second birthday, 14 April 1859.

shock was terrible, for she had lost the one person who understood her 'tomboy' pursuits, while to Louise, Albert's death and the new gloomy life they all now led meant that she would not enjoy the glamorous side of Court life. Arthur, then a boy of eleven, suffered in another way for the Queen thought him 'so like dearest Papa' that he was the one kept back to comfort his mother. The effect on Leopold was devastating because only Albert had really understood him and treated him as a normal member of the family. Yet Albert's death had the greatest effect on Beatrice. Her mother believed that Beatrice was her only reason for living, 'the only one who needs me now'. In reality, it was the reverse and the Queen was determined that 'Baby' should stay with her 'to be a comfort to me in old age'.

The Queen had not had a happy childhood, but through Albert, she had enjoyed a second childhood. Still being quite young, she could delight in the constant amusements he provided for his children. Through him, she could enjoy her children and, although she could not be described as maternal, she was, at least, a loving and giving mother. The moment Albert died, everything changed. She became introverted and selfish towards her children, critical of her sons and largely alienated herself from all their affections. It was only with the birth of her grandchildren and great-grandchildren that she began to recover those maternal instincts.

Albert, according to the historian, Roger Fulford, 'treated his children as intelligent human beings, with the dignity to which they were entitled, avoiding the boisterous chaff—crushing to the youthful spirits—with which King Edward VII was to treat his own offspring.' On the other hand, Edward has enjoyed the reputation of being a benevolent and amiable father to his five children, who made every effort to ensure that they did not suffer as he had at the hands of his father. Both views were correct. When he was in a rage, his children suffered terribly, but when in a good mood, there was no better father.

Albert Edward, Prince of Wales, son of 'the Grandmother of Europe', married Princess Alexandra, daughter of King Christian IX of Denmark, the 'Grandfather of Europe', on 10 March 1863. He was twenty-one and his bride just eighteen. Although an arranged marriage, it was a love match which certainly benefited the Prince of Wales. His mother wrote, 'we must be thankful in Bertie's so-improved and altered conduct and, in his happy marriage with dear Alix who is a *most* noble, excellent, dear creature we have a realisation of what my Angel [Albert] so ardently wished.' The young Prince and Princess of Wales's first baby was born two months prematurely on 8 January 1864. That winter was particularly fierce and the lake at Frogmore, where they were staying, was frozen over. As the Princess was pregnant she did not skate, but insisted on being taken to Virginia Water nearby to be pushed along the ice on a sledge-chair. They returned at dusk and Lady Macclesfield, the Princess's lady-in-waiting, realised that Alexandra was about to go into labour. Nothing had been prepared and Lady Macclesfield herself went into Windsor to fetch the town doctor and to buy some yards of flannel from the local draper. The Prince stayed with his wife throughout, and her baby was successfully delivered by the doctor and Lady Macclesfield, who even had to use her own petticoat as a 'receiving flannel'.

Despite the premature birth, the baby, who weighed $3\frac{3}{4}$ pounds, and his mother did well. After a slight contretemps with Queen Victoria over the choice of names, the boy was christened Albert Christian Victor Edward, but was known simply as 'Eddy'.

Eighteen months later, on 3 June 1865, the Princess of Wales gave birth to a second son at Marlborough House in London. He was born a month premature, although the genial Prince Alfred, 'Affie', remarked, 'Pray tell me, it was just at the right time was it not?' After the usual wrangle with the Queen over names, he was christened George Frederick Ernest Albert, but to all his family he was called Georgie.

Being so close in age, the boys were brought up very much together as were their three sisters, Louise, Victoria and Maud, born at regular sixteen-month intervals from 1867 onwards. In 1871, the Princess of Wales was pregnant for the last time, eight years after the birth of Eddy, and at Sandringham on 6 April, she gave birth to her third son. It was another premature birth and again nothing had been prepared. The sickly baby only lived for a day and was christened Alexander John Charles Albert shortly before he died. To the family, he was always referred to as John. He was buried below the wall of Sandringham Church. Today, in the same churchyard, there are three tragic tombstones bearing the name John, one to the thirteen-year-old son of George V and the other to the brother of the present Princess of Wales, who also lived only a day.

Apart from their father's rages, 'the Wales's', as the children were invariably known, had a happy and carefree childhood. Although they were all much in awe of their father, he provided a boisterous and close-knit family life. He cared deeply for his children and his affection was reciprocated. Princess Alexandra herself had had an enchanted childhood and she was determined that her children should be equally happy. She succeeded almost too well, denying them nothing. They called her 'Darling Motherdear', a term they used even as adults. Later in their marriage, when her philandering husband began to seek the company of other women, Alexandra turned even more to her children for solace and affection.

For most of their childhood, 'the Wales's' were predominately brought up at Sandringham, the Norfolk house bought by Queen Victoria as a wedding present for their parents. They visited London, staying at Marlborough House, Frogmore in Windsor Great Park, Abergeldie (next to Balmoral) or Osborne, to visit Queen Victoria. It was at Sandringham that Alexandra managed to reconcile the two sides of her life—providing a home for her children and a place for her wayward husband to entertain his 'fast' friends. She seems to have coped, for she was as happy bathing her children herself as she was entertaining those guests.

The children were allowed to run wild and it was that unprecedented behaviour of Eddy and Georgie, then aged eight and nearly seven, that prompted Queen Victoria to write, 'they are such ill-bred, ill-trained children I can't fancy them at all'. A frequent visitor to Sandringham, Lady Geraldine Somerset, found them 'as wild as hawks' while 'the boys were past all management'. The girls, Louise, Victoria and Maud, were variously described as 'rampaging little girls', and Victoria, or 'Toria' as she was known, was 'very sharp, quick merry and amusing'. Although Queen Victoria often found her grandchildren taxing, she was however, often amused by their pranks. Once, Georgie was sent under the table in disgrace for misbehaving at a family lunch. When he appeared again, he had removed all his clothes, to the delight of the old Queen. Their father encouraged them in their boisterous behaviour; he saw in it his own brand of humour. Once he wrote to Georgie describing some house party where he and Alexandra squirted each other with soda-syphons—a prediliction inherited by the present Prince of Wales.

The nursery for 'the Wales's' was no less amusing. Their first nurse, a Mrs Blackburn, known as Mary, was replaced by a nursery-governess, Miss Brown,

27. The Princess of Wales (later Queen Alexandra) with her children. On her left are the Princesses Louise and Maud, her right, Princes Albert Victor (Eddy) and George (Georgie) while Princess Victoria is on the floor.

who stayed on to teach the girls. Shortly after Eddy was born, a nursery-footman, Charles Fuller, was engaged. He was devoted to both boys, serving Eddy for most of his life and remaining one of Georgie's closest friends.

The Prince of Wales left the education of Eddy and Georgie until they were seven and nearly six and for that role he appointed the Reverend John Dalton as tutor. Dalton was an excellent choice with a fine academic background and a genuine interest in his two pupils and their welfare. He was to remain tutor to one or other of them for fourteen years and his friendship with Georgie lasted until he died in 1931, aged over ninety.

The daily routine set out by Dalton was thorough. Rising at seven o'clock, the boys had geography and English lessons before breakfast. Breakfast was followed by Bible study or a history lesson with algebra or Euclid at nine. After an hour's break for games, there was either a French or Latin lesson which took them up to lunch at two o'clock. They could ride or play cricket in the afternoons until tea, which was followed by more English lessons, sometimes music but always preparation. Bed was at eight when their parents, when at home, would hear their prayers and tuck them up for the night.

Every week, Dalton submitted a written report on Eddy and Georgie's work to their parents. Similar accounts of lack of concentration and application, sometimes temper, of the Prince of Wales as a boy, appeared in his sons' *Journal of Weekly Work*;

> Week ending September 2, 1876. Prince G. this week has been much troubled by silly fretfulness of temper and general spirit of contradiction.
> September 23. Prince George has been good this week. He shows however too much disposition to find fault with his brother.
> December 9. The slightest difficulty discourages him and when he frets, he finds it hard to subdue himself.

Dalton persevered with his pupils, and won through with Georgie in the end. Georgie had much to thank him for as it was he who instilled that unswerving sense of duty which was to sustain him throughout his life.

When the boys were at Marlborough House, an army sergeant drilled them every morning, then they had gymnastics and fencing instruction. They were taught to ride at the Knightsbridge Barracks and joined their sisters for their dancing lessons and tennis and croquet coaching. Georgie showed particular aptitude for shooting and later became one of the finest shots in the country.

Dalton could see the dangers of the confined atmosphere in which the children were brought up. Apart from the family and their parents' close friends, the members of the Household and servants, they saw no one. Together they were uninhibited, but with strangers they became shy and gauche, the girls being called 'the whispering Wales's'. They had next to no education, apart from music, and only Maud inherited any of their mother's good looks.

After six years of Dalton's patient teaching, the Prince of Wales decided that it was time that Eddy and Georgie, then aged thirteen and nearly twelve, should

28. The Prince of Wales's two sons, Prince Albert Victor and Prince George, on board HMS *Britannia*, December 1877.

The Royal Family

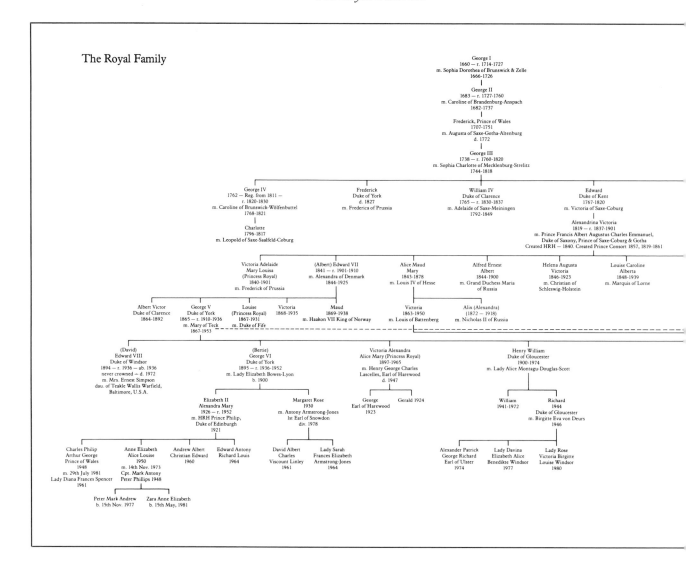

George I
1660 — r. 1714-1727
m. Sophia Dorothea of Brunswick & Zelle
1666-1726

George II
1683 — r. 1727-1760
m. Caroline of Brandenburg-Anspach
1682-1737

Frederick, Prince of Wales
1707-1751
m. Augusta of Saxe-Gotha-Altenburg
d. 1772

George III
1738 — r. 1760-1820
m. Sophia Charlotte of Mecklenburg-Strelitz
1744-1818

George IV
1762 — Reg. from 1811 —
r. 1820-1830
m. Caroline of Brunswick-Wölfenbuttel
1768-1821

Frederick
Duke of York
d. 1827
m. Frederica of Prussia

William IV
Duke of Clarence
1765 — r. 1830-1837
m. Adelaide of Saxe-Meiningen
1792-1849

Edward
Duke of Kent
1767-1820
m. Victoria of Saxe-Coburg

Charlotte
1796-1817
m. Leopold of Saxe-Saalfeld-Coburg

Alexandrina Victoria
1819 — r. 1837-1901
m. Prince Francis Albert Augustus Charles Emmanuel,
Duke of Saxony, Prince of Saxe-Coburg & Gotha
Created HRH — 1840. Created Prince Consort 1857, 1819-1861

Victoria Adelaide
Mary Louisa
(Princess Royal)
1840-1901
m. Frederick of Prussia

(Albert) Edward VII
1841 — r. 1901-1910
m. Alexandra of Denmark
1844-1925

Alice Maud
Mary
1843-1878
m. Louis IV of Hesse

Alfred Ernest
Albert
1844-1900
m. Grand Duchess Maria
of Russia

Helena Augusta
Victoria
1846-1923
m. Christian of
Schleswig-Holstein

Louise Caroline
Alberta
1848-1939
m. Marquis of Lorne

Albert Victor
Duke of Clarence
1864-1892

George V
Duke of York
1865 — r. 1910-1936
m. Mary of Teck
1867-1953

Louise
(Princess Royal)
1867-1931
m. Duke of Fife

Victoria
1868-1935

Maud
1869-1938
m. Haakon VII King of Norway

Victoria
1863-1950
m. Louis of Battenberg

Alix (Alexandra)
(1872 — 1918)
m. Nicholas II of Russia

(David)
Edward VIII
Duke of Windsor
1894 — r. 1936 — ab. 1936
never crowned — d. 1972
m. Mrs. Ernest Simpson
dau. of Teakle Wallis Warfield,
Baltimore, U.S.A.

(Bertie)
George VI
Duke of York
1895 — r. 1936-1952
m. Lady Elizabeth Bowes-Lyon
b. 1900

Victoria Alexandra
Alice Mary (Princess Royal)
1897-1965
m. Henry George Charles
Lascelles, Earl of Harewood
d. 1947

Henry William
Duke of Gloucester
1900-1974
m. Lady Alice Montagu-Douglas-Scott

Elizabeth II
Alexandra Mary
1926 — r. 1952
m. HRH Prince Philip,
Duke of Edinburgh
1921

Margaret Rose
1930
m. Antony Armstrong-Jones
1st Earl of Snowdon
div. 1978

George
Earl of Harewood
1923

Gerald 1924

William
1941-1972

Richard
1944
Duke of Gloucester
m. Birgitte Eva von Deurs
1946

Charles Philip
Arthur George
Prince of Wales
1948
m. 29th July 1981
Lady Diana Frances Spencer
1961

Anne Elizabeth
Alice Louise
1950
m. 14th Nov. 1973
Cpt. Mark Antony
Peter Phillips 1948

Andrew Albert
Christian Edward
1960

Edward Antony
Richard Louis
1964

David Albert
Charles
Viscount Linley
1961

Lady Sarah
Frances Elizabeth
Armstrong-Jones
1964

Alexander Patrick
George Richard
Earl of Ulster
1974

Lady Davina
Elizabeth Alice
Benedikte Windsor
1977

Lady Rose
Victoria Birgitte
Louise Windsor
1980

Peter Mark Andrew
b. 15th Nov. 1977

Zara Anne Elizabeth
b. 15th May, 1981

have a broader education. As the younger son, Georgie was always destined for the Navy and the training ship *Britannia* was the first step in his career. The Queen wanted Eddy to go to Wellington, a boys' public school in which Prince Albert had taken an interest. But Dalton could see the disadvantages of splitting up the two brothers. Although devoted companions, they were very different in character. Of the two, Georgie was the brighter, 'a jolly little pickle', and not unintelligent. By contrast, Eddy was 'apathetic, backward, lacking in manliness and self-reliance, an almost impossible subject for education.' His easy nature appealed to his mother and sisters but his lackadaisical manner infuriated his father.

Dalton finally had his way and Georgie sat and passed, to his tutor's delight,

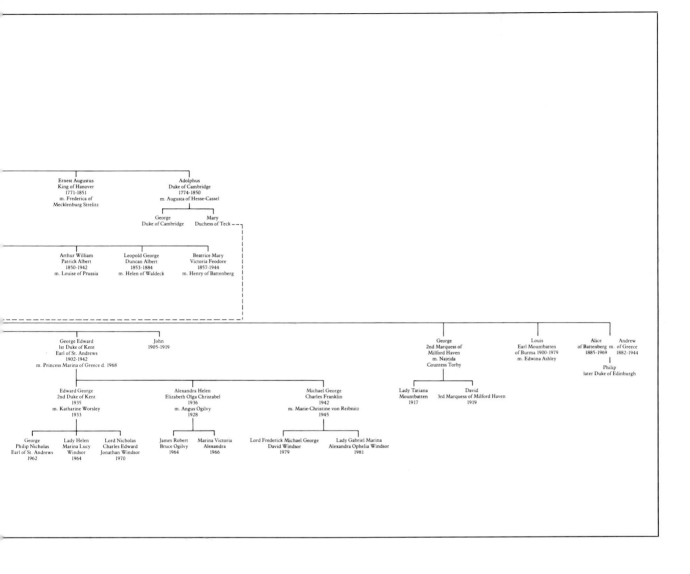

into *Britannia*. In September 1877, Georgie, accompanied by Eddy and Dalton, joined the training ship. Apart from a cabin to themselves, the Princes were treated exactly as the other cadets. Georgie did well on *Britannia*, but his brother's standard of intelligence was so low that the Captain Superintendant recommended that he be removed. The Prince and Princess of Wales were greatly distressed that their son, who, on the death of Queen Victoria, would be heir to the throne, was so totally backward. After two years on *Brittannia*, Georgie, at the age of fourteen, passed out quite creditably. Next, he joined a Navy training ship for a lengthy cruise. Dalton again advised that the brothers be kept together so Georgie joined HMS *Bacchante* for a three-year world cruise accompanied by both Eddy and the long-suffering Dalton. While Georgie made 'rapid and pronounced progress', easily passing his midshipman's exams, Eddy again lagged far behind.

That difference between the brothers was to continue all their lives, although their affection for each other never altered. George went on to forge a career for himself in the Navy while his feckless brother never settled down to anything. When Eddy died of pneumonia at the age of twenty-eight in 1892, the line of royal descent took another another twist as George became the heir to the throne. By the time George married and had children of his own, Queen Victoria was still on the throne, and in the last years of her life, she was still able to exert her considerable influence on the way in which her great-grandchildren were brought up.

2

King George V and his Children

In the middle of Ascot Week, 1894, the Prince of Wales hosted a ball in the Fishing Temple beside Virginia Water in Windsor Great Park. The Prince strode over to the orchestra and, as the strains of the music faded over the water, he made the announcement, 'It is with pleasure that I am able to inform you of the birth of a son to the Duke and Duchess of York. I propose a toast to the young prince.'

For the six weeks of the confinement, the Duke and Duchess of York had been staying with the Duchess's parents, the Duke and Duchess of Teck, at White Lodge, a fine and commodious Georgian house in Richmond Park. The Duke spent the evening of the birth reading *Pilgrim's Progress* as he waited nervously for his first-born child. He need not have worried because all went well and he subsequently recorded in his dairy: 'WHITE LODGE, 23rd June—At 10.0 a sweet little boy was born and weighed 8 lb'.

The Duke of York's life had changed dramatically with the death of his brother, the Duke of Clarence, in January 1892. Until then, George was third in line to the throne after his father, the Prince of Wales [Edward VII], and his brother. He had had a promising career, having risen both by dint of hard work and by merit to the rank of captain in the Royal Navy. When 'dearest Eddy' died, he had to abandon the sea and concentrate on affairs of State which were totally alien to him. In July 1893, he married his late brother's fiancée, Princess May of Teck, whom he had known all his life. The Duke declared that he could only love a woman who could reciprocate his love and, although their's was the last arranged marriage of a future English monarch, it was happy and secure.

The baby was christened Edward Albert Christian George Andrew Patrick David. The choice of names was tact itself: Edward after his grandfather, late uncle and six past kings; Albert in deference to Queen Victoria's wish that all her British descendants should bear the name of her beloved husband; Christian after his Danish grandfather; while the rest of the names were the patron saints of England, Scotland, Ireland and Wales respectively. Despite this rich nomenclature, he was known by his family and friends as David. Queen Victoria attended the christening in the Chapel Royal at St James's Palace and was one of

29. Four generations of monarchs and three successive Princes of Wales. Queen Victoria holds Prince Edward (David), wearing the traditional Honiton Lace robes at his christening in 1894. She is flanked by her son, later Edward VII, and his son, later George V.

his many sponsors. She recorded the event in her diary, ending: 'Had tea with Mary [Duchess of York], and afterwards we were photographed, I holding the baby on my lap, Bertie and Georgie standing behind me, thus making four generations.'

Home to the Duke and Duchess of York was then York Cottage, a small and uninspiring house in the grounds of Sandringham House in Norfolk. The house remained the favourite of the Duke for thirty-three years but it is doubtful if any of his family shared his attachment. His biographer, Sir Harold Nicholson, describes it as:

> A glum little villa encompassed by thickets of laurel and rhododendron, shadowed by huge Wellingtonias and separated by an abrupt rim of lawn from a pond at the edge of which a leaden pelican gazes in dejection upon the water lilies and bamboos. The rooms inside, with their fumed oak surrounds, their white overmantels framing oval mirrors, their Doulton tiles and stained-glass fanlights, are indistinguishable from any Surbiton or Upper Norwood home. The Duke's own sitting-room, its north window blocked by heavy shrubberies, was rendered even darker by the red cloth covering which saddened the walls.

To add to the acute discomfort, the plumbing in that 'most undesirable residence' was basic and there were too few bathrooms. Although the bedrooms of the Duke and Duchess of York were of a good size, the rest were poky and small—the lady-in-waiting's room, for example, being a cubicle over the butler's pantry. The Duke said that he thought 'the servants slept in the trees', and before a meal, the whole house reeked of cooking.

The house had been a wedding present from his father and, to save his bride the trouble, the Duke of York had furnished it with the help of someone he called the 'Maples Man'. Years later, his eldest son wrote: 'Until you have seen York Cottage, you will never understand my father.' The cramped quarters, the smell, the discomfort, and the austere, funereal decoration, must have been as near as it was possible to get on land to the atmosphere of a Royal Navy ship.

It was at York Cottage, on 14 December 1895, that the Duke and Duchess of York's second son was born. The confinement was easy and the birth straightforward. The Duke wrote in his diary, 'a little boy was born weighing nearly eight lbs at 3.30 S.T. Everything most satisfactory, both doing well.' The S.T. referred to Sandringham Time as the Duke, a stickler for punctuality, kept all the clocks half-an-hour fast.

It was, however, an unfortunate day to be born in royal circles for it was the anniversary of the death of not only the 'beloved Albert' but also the Queen's second daughter, Alice. Indeed, the Queen was reported to be 'rather distressed' that day, but before long she mellowed, particularly when she heard that the new baby was to be called Albert. As a christening present, she donated a bust of the late Prince Consort, although she was too infirm to travel to Sandringham for the christening itself. As the baby received the names Albert Frederick Arthur George, he began to yell and David, aged only eighteen months, who up to then

30. York Cottage, the favourite home at Sandringham, Norfolk, of King George V,
where all his children were brought up

had watched the ceremony in intrigued silence, began to scream in sympathy and had to be removed.

Life started badly in the nursery for the infant brothers. The first head-nurse had to be dismissed for insolence and the replacement had a nervous breakdown—it was discovered afterwards that she had not had a day off in three years. She was 'sadistic and incompetent' and it remains a mystery how she held her position for so long undetected. Although she adored David she was jealous of his natural affections for his parents. Before taking David and Bertie, in their white dresses, into the drawing-room, she would pinch David or twist his arm to make him scream. The sobbing child would then be instantly banished with orders for his nurse to soothe him. She totally ignored Bertie, maybe even mistreated him. The stomach trouble that was to dog Bertie all his life has partly been attributed to the nurse giving him his bottle in a victoria—a sprung four-wheeled carriage with a particularly sick-making, rolling movement. That nurse was replaced by Mrs Bill, the loveable 'Lalla', who had been promoted from under-nurse.

The third child was born on 25 April 1897 at York Cottage. Her arrival was doubly happy since, after two boys, she was a girl and she was born in the

Queen's Jubilee year. The Queen crowed, 'My dear little Jubilee baby', but the Prince of Wales's suggestion that she be called 'Diamond' was not accepted by the parents. She was in fact christened Victoria Alexandra Alice Mary, but to the family she was always known as Mary. Thus the first 'stage' of the York's family, all born within a three-year span, was complete. A nursery wing was added onto the house where the three children lived with their staff.

The nursery life of the 'Happy Trio', as their mother called them, was typical of any upper-class family of the age. The nanny took total charge of the children providing them with a basic education and the all-important 'sense of duty'. The York children flourished in the care of Mrs Bill who ruled her nursery with a blend of love and discipline. The children's relationship with their parents was somewhat different. Whenever possible, the Duke and Duchess would be at York Cottage. They would receive their children washed and wearing white dresses, for tea. Their father claimed that 'he got on with children like a house on fire' but, in common with other Victorian fathers, they were 'other people's children'. Outwardly he was a model family man. He would bath his children, weigh them and on odd occasions play with them. Yet he remained a remote, aloof figure. His unpredictable temper tended to distance him from his children and, although they were devoted to their father, they were much in awe of him and not a little frightened, as Nicholson observed. 'His manner of chaffing them or interrogating them added to the shyness and tied the tongues of those by nature the most diffident and the same qualities that gained him the devotion of his staff and servants and the admiration of his wider family as their ideal head, sometimes created a barrier which separated him from his own sons.' The countess of Airlie, a lady-in-waiting and friend of the Duchess of York, added that the Duke and Duchess

> have often been depicted as stern unloving parents, but this they most certainly were not. . . . I believe they were more conscientious and more truly devoted to their children than the majority of parents in that era. The tragedy was that neither of them had any understanding of a child's mind. They themselves had been brought up in particularly loving homes . . . but they did not succeed in making their own children happy.

Also, the Duchess found it difficult to intercede between her husband, when he was in a foul temper, and their children.

In the nursery, the three children suffered from the lack of outside friends and the remoteness of their parents. Often with threesomes, there is an odd one out, and with that trio it was the middle child, Bertie. He was a shy boy, easily frightened and prone to fits of crying, whereas David was robust and confident and Mary, her father's favourite, had 'that little girl charm'. Consequently, Bertie tended to shrink into the background, often being ignored altogether. Queen Victoria known to all her grandchildren as 'Gangan', recorded one of their visits: 'The dear little York children came, looking very well. David is a delightful child, so intelligent, nice and friendly. The baby is a sweet pretty little

31. Princes Edward and Albert (David and Bertie) with a toy horse and cart at
Osborne on the Isle of Wight. *c.* 1897.

thing.' But, although he was present, too, she made no mention of Bertie.

David, by his age, size and personality, was the leader of the 'Trio'. He, in
turn, was devoted to his sister, an affection that was reciprocated with
something approaching hero-worship. Bertie, too, was close to his sister and he
followed his brother with dogged admiration into every conceivable sort of
trouble, for which he invariably took the blame. With such a reputation for
naughtiness, he was often singled out for the most punishment and criticism.
Even his birthday greeting from his father contained a stern warning: 'Now that
you are five years old, I hope you will try & be obedient & do at once what you
are told.'

'The Happy Trio' became a quartet on 31 March 1900 with the birth of Henry
William Frederick Albert. The Duchess wrote to her Aunt Augusta, 'I confess I
am just a little proud of myself for having produced another boy which was
greatly wished for . . . The children are so pleased with the baby who they think
flew in at my window & had to have his wings cut off.'

While York Cottage was home, the children spent much of their time in other
royal houses. They followed the royal migration to London, where they stayed at
York House, or to Windsor where they lived at Frogmore House, an elegant
cream-coloured mansion in the Park. Sometimes they went to Osborne, an

8. Queen Victoria at the age of eleven, with her dog, 'Fanny', painted by her drawing master, R. Westall RA, for her mother the Duchess of Kent in 1827.

9. The younger children of King George V and Queen Mary fishing at Abergeldie, Scotland, 1911. From left to right, Princess Mary, Princes John, George, Henry and Albert.

10. The Prince of Wales, later Edward VIII, as a Naval Cadet at Dartmouth, 1911.

11. Princess Elizabeth in the syringa at Windsor Castle, July 1941.

12. Queen Elizabeth with her daughters, Princesses Elizabeth and Margaret, in the
garden at Windsor Castle, July 1941.

32. King George V, as Duke of York, with his three eldest children, Princes Albert and Edward and Princess Mary. The photograph was taken by Alexandra, Princess of Wales, on board HMS *Osborne* in August 1899.

imitation Italian villa on the Isle of Wight, and to Scotland to stay at Abergeldie Castle on the Balmoral estate.

At home, their life was spent mostly out of doors. They knew every inch of the Sandringham estate, the woods, the tenant farms, the game-keepers' pens and the kennels that housed fifty assorted dogs and hounds. They climbed trees and went birds'-nesting and rode their bicycles to the village shops to buy sweets or over to watch the trains at Wolferton station. London held different attractions. The children loved to see troops being drilled in Hyde Park or marching behind brass bands, soldiers who were shortly to be drafted to South Africa and the Boer War.

Frogmore House was another good place to visit with its long, wide avenues and open drives, the sweeping lawns and the lake below—a young bicyclist's paradise. When they were older, they would row on the River Thames or go for picnics in the electrically-powered launch. Grand though the house looked, it, too, lacked comfort as a royal residence—for instance, there was only one bathroom situated on the ground floor for family and guests alike.

Best of all were the annual visits to Scotland for the summer. Great excitement preceded their departure by overnight train to the little station of Ballater, followed by the drive to Abergeldie, a fourteenth-century castle not far from Balmoral. There they were completely free and could run wild. There was always much to do on the estate, many places to explore. There were picnics and walks—their favourite being across the foot-suspension bridge over the River Dee on a windy day. There were endless bicycle rides, puffing up the steep Deeside hills and freewheeling down the other side, crouched low over the handlebars. When they were older, they were taught to shoot and to fish. In the castle itself there was the exciting thought of meeting the ghost of a woman, Kittie Rankie, who had been burned as a witch on a nearby hilltop.

The real trial was staying at Osborne during Queen Victoria's lifetime and they would dissolve into tears whenever they saw 'Gangan'. Their behaviour annoyed the old woman who repeatedly asked them what they had done wrong. On 22 January 1901, Queen Victoria died at Osborne. The children were then at York Cottage in quarantine for German measles but David, Bertie and Mary were allowed to go to Windsor for the funeral. They attended the ceremony in St George's Chapel at Windsor Castle and two days later they joined the throng of crowned heads of Europe, princes and other dignitaries at the interment at the mausoleum at Frogmore. It was a bitterly cold day and the two brothers stood patiently amongst sobbing relatives in deep mourning.

Their grandfather now became King Edward VII, and the effect was soon felt in the nursery at York Cottage, for their parents were sent on a prolonged Empire Tour to Australia. The parting was a great wrench. Although David was nearly seven, Henry was still under a year old, and as they said goodbye, Mary threw her arms around her mother's neck and said in her high-pitched voice, 'Never mind, I will take good care of us!' Their father enjoined that his children should write to him throughout the tour. Bertie's first letter was written and posted to

Gibraltar four days before they left:

> MY DARLING MAMA AND PAPA,
> We hope you are quite well and not seasick. Did you have a big wave when you
> went through the bay of Biscay?
> We send you love and lots of kisses,
>   From your loving,
>   Bertie.

Nursery life for the royal children was certainly more relaxed and considerably more fun without their parents. Their nanny, 'Lalla', had been joined by a governess, Mlle Hélène Brika. This plump and aged woman from Alsace had taught their mother as a girl and now attempted to instruct the three unruly pupils. Their natural preference for fun rather than learning was supported by the King and Queen Alexandra, who spoilt them incessantly. They encouraged their boisterous natures and allowed them to romp at all times, even in the dining-room when they had important guests. In that happy atmosphere, it was all too easy to forget afternoon lessons, and once when Mlle Brika came to fetch them, she was waved aside by the King who said 'It's all right, let the children stay with us a little longer. We shall send them upstairs presently.' The children went with their grandparents on their round of houses for the eight months the Duke and Duchess were abroad, and on one occasion when they went to Sandringham, Mlle Brika was left behind in case she spoiled the fun.

Not surprisingly, the Duke and Duchess of York were horrified by their childrens' behaviour on their return from Australia and the Duke realised that his sons could no longer be controlled by women. 'Lalla' Bill stayed on to care for Mary and Henry while Frederick Finch would take over the boys. Finch, who had been promoted from nursery-footman, was about thirty and 'handsome, stalwart and muscular, naturally respectful but without a trace of servility'. Initially, he acted as a male nursemaid, attending to their clothes, polishing their shoes, as well as fulfilling duties like saying prayers with them or tucking them up in bed—even beating them when the occasion arose. He was the boys' greatest ally and their devotion was total. Later Finch's rôle grew to one of arbiter, confidant and companion, and was to stay with David in later life, first as valet, then butler right up to his retirement.

The next change in their routine came in the spring of 1902. One morning the boys heard the ominous footfall of their father outside their rooms in York House. They waited terrified as the door opened to reveal their father standing outside with a 'tall, gaunt, solemn stranger with a large moustache'. 'This is Mr Hansell, your new tutor,' he declared coldly before walking away leaving the stranger behind. Henry Peter Hansell was their father's obvious choice as tutor, being of good Norfolk stock, a former preparatory and minor public school-master and a fair sportsman. Years later, David wrote of him as combining 'a mild scholarship with a muscular Christianity, accentuated by tweeds and an ever-present pipe'. He was soon called 'Mider'—a mispronunciation of 'Mister'. For

David and Bertie, the arrival of Hansell was a shock. Their lessons before had been somewhat erratic and now Hansell tried to create a classroom atmosphere in the new schoolroom at York Cottage with a blackboard and two plain school desks. Their timetable was similar to a preparatory school—up at 7 am, 'prep' between 7.30 and 8.15 before breakfast, and lessons between 9 am and 1 pm and for an hour before tea. Occasionally, the boys were sent off to play football with the village children, but neither side enjoyed the experience.

Meanwhile, in the nursery below the schoolroom, Mary played with the youngest brother, Henry, until she could join David and Bertie when they had finished their lessons. She was an enchanting child with large blue eyes and a shock of fair curls. Henry, on the other hand was a more difficult child and showed a volatile temper. Once, when barely two years old, he was forced, wearing a stiff white petticoat, in a foul mood, into the dining-room to meet an aged great-aunt. 'The Grand-Duchess bent her face down and asked him if he could not say anything to her: would he not at all events give Aunt Augusta a kiss? Before one could say anything, there was a sharp sound, and a little hand had inflicted a sharp slap on the Grand-Duchess's cheek.'

In the spring of 1902, the Duke of York was created Prince of Wales and the whole household, including the schoolroom, moved to York House. Their move coincided with the intense excitement over the preparations for the Coronation scheduled for the end of June. Hansell used the occasion to bring to life his history lessons and took the boys and their sister to Westminster Abbey to see the Coronation chair and to the Tower of London to see the Crown Jewels. In contrast to the experience of today's royal children, David, Bertie and Mary could walk around the streets of London with their tutor completely at ease. There were few photographs in those days and they were rarely recognised from the sketches in magazines. Other 'treats' included visits to the zoo, to Madame Tussaud's, to the Natural History Museum and, to indulge Hansell's love of church architecture, to innumerable churches.

King Edward VII was crowned on 9 August 1902. David, Bertie and Mary witnessed the ceremony, the boys wearing 'Balmoral costume' (kilts). They sat in a box reserved for Princesses of the Royal Blood, under the watchful eyes of Hansel and Finch. They fidgeted throughout the long ceremony and whispered incessantly. At the most solemn part of the ceremony, one of their great-aunts dropped her heavily embossed Order of Service over the edge of the box to the howling delight of the children—for which, later, their father strongly reproved them.

Having sworn that she would have no more children, the Princess of Wales proceeded to have another two boys. Their fifth child, George Edward Alexander Edmund of Wales, was born just before Christmas, on 20 December 1902, at York Cottage and, finally, John Charles Francis was born three years later. From the moment of their births , their lives followed an identical pattern to their four brothers and sister with the same nursery, nursery staff and routine.

As all the children grew up, their relationship with their father grew even more remote. His treatment of his sons was likened to the captain of a cruiser with midshipmen—both were noisy young nuisances in constant need of correction. The summons, 'His Royal Highness wishes to see you in the Library', struck terror into them all. On the other hand, their mother's room became a kind of sanctuary in which, at the end of the day, she would read to her children or teach them to crochet, knit or embroider. The Princess of Wales was a fine needlewoman and passed on her skill not only to Mary but also to all her sons. At the Needlework Guild, a member remarked on the neatness of one of Mary's canvasses to which her mother replied, 'Yes, I am afraid they cost some tears, for dropped stitches had to be picked up'.

Much to the childrens' dislike, more and more of their time was spent in London. In the spring of 1903, the Prince of Wales and his growing family moved into Marlborough House. The move suited the Princess who preferred the grander surroundings but her children missed the open spaces of their other homes. At that point the Princess decided that her children should lose some of their rustic habits and that the cure would be dancing lessons. The result was a class for about twenty-five contemporaries of the three oldest children, held twice a week in the dining-room of Marlborough House under the expert guidance of a Miss Walsh. They could hardly be described as fun but at least the children met other children of their own age.

To a great extent, however, David, Bertie, Mary and later Henry continued to turn to the royal household for companionship. To keep alive a family tradition, their father had taken on two Scots ex-servicemen, Henry Forsyth and Findlay Cameron, to act as valet and piper. Every morning at exactly eight o'clock the Prince of Wales was woken by the skirl of the pipes below his window and sometimes guests were treated to some Scottish airs during dinner. The three small boys, as well as their sister, were greatly attracted to Forsyth and Cameron. Forsyth had been a pipe-major in the Scots Guards and Cameron had served with the Queen's Own Cameron Highlanders for twenty-one years. He was a master of self-glorification and regaled the children with stirring stories of his many campaigns, the hand-to-hand fighting with the 'Fuzzy-Wuzzies', or the desperate last stand in some Boer skirmish. Seeing their passionate interest in the Changing of the Guard and all things military, Cameron organised the four children into a drill squad. They paraded every day with wooden rifles and, led by Forsyth with his pipes, were drilled by Cameron. They enjoyed it enormously, particularly at Sandringham when their grandfather came to inspect them.

The constant migrations of the Royal Family continued, the Prince of Wales, with or without his family, always close in attendance on his father the King. Christmas was always spent at Sandringham and the children would stay on until March with their tutor. As the boys grew older, Mr Hansell was joined by other tutors. Monsieur Gabriel Hua had taught French to the Prince of Wales and was brought back into royal service after eighteen years as a master at Eton, Dr

33. Parade for Princes Edward, Albert and Henry and Princess Mary, with Cameron the piper and Forsyth, the drill sergeant.

Oswald taught the boys German, and Martin David taught mathematics. Hansell saw himself as a headmaster and left strict instruction to his aides as to how their charges fared. Failure to 'come up to the mark' resulted, even for the favourite daughter Mary, in a visit to the 'Library'.

Discipline varied in the schoolroom. Once, Dr Oswald complained to the Prince of Wales of Bertie's lack of concentration during his lessons. He had also had to admit that not only was Bertie inattentive 'but when I scold him he just pulls my beard'. Mary joined the schoolroom only briefly as her presence was thought to be disruptive. Hansell reported, 'I must keep Princess Mary apart from the others as much as possible. . . . Her disposition is mercurial; one can enforce discipline and order of a sort but the fact remains that, so long as she is in the room, her brothers cannot concentrate their attention on any serious work'.

Mary was withdrawn from the school-room and put under her own governess, Mademoiselle José Dussau. She was quick and intelligent for her age, a good linguist and often took the lead in the classroom over her slower brothers. She had her own schoolroom and when in London shared lesson with the Duke of Devonshire's younger daughters—a class dubbed 'the flapper brigade' by her

34. Princes Edward and Albert with their French tutor, M. Hua, 1903.

brother David. She was also an excellent rider, far better than her brothers, and would ride every morning before breakfast for half-an-hour.

Bertie, on the other hand, was not so fortunate. He had developed a dreadful stammer, the cause attributed to being forced to write with his right hand while being naturally left-handed. He was a highly-strung, sensitive child, prone to fits of uncontrollable anger or depression. His own shortcomings annoyed him and only served to heighten his temper. His stammer tended to alienate him from his parents, brothers and sister, for he was unable to compete in the inevitable family banter and the childrens' mimicry of him distressed him further. It is no wonder that he alternated between lapses of concentration, outbursts of exuberance and deep depression and sobbing. If that was not enough for the little Prince to bear he had, in common with Henry, knock knees. His father, with the same complaint, asked his physician to design splints for his sons. Bertie found them painful to wear and Hansell thought they detracted from his concentration. Certainly his work suffered, so it was decided that the splints need only be worn at night. Once, Bertie pleaded with Finch not to fit them onto his legs as they were so painful. Finch relented, only to be summoned to the

Library by the Prince of Wales. The Prince drew his trousers close to his legs and bellowed, 'Look at me. If that boy grows up to look like this, it will be your fault.'

When the Prince and Princess of Wales went on their tour of Australia, they left behind four children with the youngest of one year. When they left for a State visit to India in October 1905 there were six children, the youngest only three months—John, their last child, had been born on 12 July at York Cottage.

Once again the régime at York Cottage was relaxed in the absence of the Prince and Princess of Wales, although the King, with increased responsibilities, could not give them so much of his time or spoil them to the same extent as before. Even from India the Prince of Wales admonished his elder children, usually for not writing at the prescribed time. The younger children fared better, sending their love and 'the first snowdrop for dear Mama from Harry and Georgie'.

Discipline tightened on their parents' return. David had by now outgrown the schoolroom. Bertie resented his brother's superiority and both he and David knew exactly how to antagonise each other. Hansell reported, 'It is extraordinary how the presence of one acts as a sort of "red rag" to the other.' The problem was solved by David passing into the Royal Naval College at Osborne in the spring of 1907. Bertie was now the leader in the schoolroom and David's place was taken by Henry. The two had much in common. Bertie (like Prince Charles in his schooldays) found mathematics extraordinarily difficult, hated the subject and was incensed by his poor performance. His father wrote, 'You really must give up losing your temper when you make a mistake in a sum', then gave the usual advice to Hansel to be stricter. Henry was also given to the same bouts of temper over his schoolwork. Both boys suffered from severe colds, particularly Henry who was considered 'delicate'. He, too, had to wear the dreaded splints on his legs but in both cases, the severe treatment worked.

In the holidays, David returned to take up his old position as 'captain' although Mary could always assert herself when she wanted. Their mother hated sailing and did not care for shooting, so the children spent much of the summer with her on her own at Frogmore. Once, on the 'Cut', a tributary of the River Thames by Dachet, David and Bertie were rowing a scull with Mary at the helm. They collided with an Eton coxed-four. In the confusion, an Etonian shouted at Mary, 'When are you going to learn to row?', to which she, being more then their match, replied 'When you've learnt some manners!'

George was growing up and he too fell under the authority of David. In that summer a boring and pompous prince told some story to them all in the nursery. At the end, they all laughed politely except for George. 'Smile', David whispered crossly with a nudge in the ribs. The plaintive reply came, 'I can't, my face won't let me.'

Despite her five brothers, Mary never became a complete tomboy. She enjoyed working the model dairy that Queen Alexandra had set up at Sandringham. In true Marie Antoinette fashion, she would milk the cows then churn the milk, making little pats of butter for her father's breakfast. Cooking,

35. Prince Edward, kneeling in mock submission to Commander Campbell watched
by his tutor, Mr Hansell, at Frogmore House, 1907.

too, was a favourite occupation, particularly 'things I can eat myself afterwards'.
Her brother George rather sadly asked on being given one of her rock-cakes, 'As
it's a holiday, must I be polite today?'

Piano and singing were studied under a Madame Hutchinson, lessons which
she enjoyed and at which she even excelled. Mary was also the perpetrator of
most of the practical jokes within the family. One lunch-time at Frogmore,
Monsieur Hua expanded on the delights of French cuisine, in particular frogs'
legs. Mary thought she would indulge the tutor with his favourite food but
being the spawning season they had to be content with tadpoles. The cook was
instructed to boil and serve them up on toast as a special savoury for M. Hua.
Intense excitement followed as the footman laid the dish before the French tutor.

As he attacked the strange-looking concoction, the Princess of Wales, who was in on the joke, cried as he took the first mouthful, 'No, no! That special savoury is not meant to be eaten at all.' It was Mary who had to confess, whereupon M. Hua swallowed his mouthful, rose, gave a curt bow to the Princess then strode from the room. David was sent to apologise on behalf of the family and the French gourmet returned.

With a tremendous effort Bertie passed 'most creditably' into the Royal Naval College, Osborne, in November 1908. He passed his oral examination, at first stammering badly. Once he had settled down, he coped 'brightly and well'. The College provided a challenge he needed and, after an indifferent start, Bertie, who was so often unsure of himself and his ability and sometimes idle, succeeded in the end.

From the very beginning of his appointment, Hansell was against the form of education chosen by the Prince of Wales for his children. He believed that their 'walled-in' existence was wrong. If they were to be treated as ordinary cadets when they went to Osborne, they should have the same schooling as every other boy in their term—a preparatory school—to equip them for what lay ahead. Henry was more fortunate. Because of his delicate health, he was sent to his father's physician's home, York Gate House, in Broadstairs in Kent, for 'the air'. There he was looked after by Sister Edith Ward, who had nursed his father through one of his illnesses.

Henry was an emotional child, much given to uncontrollable fits of crying or giggling and Sister Edith was charged with 'the curing of this tiresome, nervous habit'. He much enjoyed his time at Broadstairs as it held untold delights for a boy of ten with a previously strict upbringing. The sands, the hunts for shells and fossils at Dumpton Gap, the walks on the esplanade and pier at Margate and the electric tram ride to Ramsgate were novel and exciting. His work fell far short of his father's exacting standard and, like his brothers before him, he came in for harsh words: ' . . . you must really do your best and be obedient & do what she [Sister Edith] tells you & not behave like a little baby . . . ' Henry's reply must have upset the Prince of Wales: 'Dear Papa, Thank you very much for your nice letter you so kindly sent me. We have got a few more good fossils for my collection . . . Best love to you all from your devoted son Harry'.

Hansell finally had his way and it was decided that Henry should go to St Peter's Court at Broadstairs. The headmaster, an acquaintance of Hansell's called A. J. Richardson, was summoned for interview to Marlborough House and it was soon agreed to send Henry as a day-boy. Henry wrote to his mother, 'I don't know whether I like the idea of going to school or not'. But he did like it and the experiment was judged a success.

On the morning of Saturday, 7 May 1910, Bertie was looking out of the schoolroom window of Marlborough House towards Buckingham Palace. The Royal Standard was flying at half-mast and, although no one had told them, he and David sensed that their beloved 'Grandpapa' was dead. Henry wrote from Broadstairs, 'I am so awfully sorry that dear Grandpapa is dead and that you

36. Henry Hansell with his two pupils, Princes Edward and Albert.

Mama, Grannie and Aunt Toria are in such trouble. I shall try to help you by being a good boy'.

From behind the garden wall at Marlborough House, David and Bertie, dressed in their uniforms of naval cadets, and George all witnessed the proclamation of the Accession of King George V from the balcony of Friary Court, St James's Palace. The three eldest children travelled in a State coach with their mother, the new Queen, behind the funeral cortège of their grandfather through the streets of London. Then David and Bertie marched with nine European sovereigns and scores of representatives from around the world behind the coffin from the station to St George's Chapel.

King George V was crowned on 22 June 1911. David, who had just left Dartmouth, had been created Prince of Wales earlier in the year. The day before the Coronation he had been invested as a Knight of the Garter so that he could wear the Garter robes and coronet of that Order. As Prince of Wales, David had his own procession and drove in a State carriage with Bertie, who was in his Dartmouth cadet's uniform, Mary in her State robes and Henry and George in Highland dress. John was considered too young and ill to attend. At Westminster Abbey the new Prince of Wales was escorted to his chair and his brothers and sister saluted him—the boys with neck bows, Mary with a low curtsey. David stood up and bowed to her in return.

The accession of King George V meant more moves for his family—from Marlborough House to Buckingham Palace, from Frogmore to Windsor Castle, from Abergeldie to Balmoral, but York Cottage was retained so that Queen Alexandra could use Sandringham as her own.

The schoolroom at Buckingham Palace was revived for Mary's lessons and for George under the perennial tutelage of Henry Hansell. Unlike his elder brothers, George was quick to learn and took an added interest in his lessons. History was a strong subject and in answer to an examination question on Perkin Warbeck, George wrote, 'He was a pretender. He pretended to be the son of a King, but he was really the son of respectable parents!' George was also the artistic member of the family and it was he who chose the decorations with such flair when the children were old enough to furnish and decorate their rooms.

Henry did much better than expected at his preparatory school although the customary letters of complaint and warning still came from his father. By the time George joined him, Henry was a senior boy and could have ignored him as was the usual form at such a school. Instead, Henry took his brother in hand, showing great kindness—so unlike his own treatment at the hands of his elder brothers. Henry had certainly made his mark at the school. He rarely excelled either academically or at sports, but what he achieved was the result of perseverance, keenness and hard work. George, by contrast, was naturally gifted and although two years younger, more than a match for his elder brother. Despite this, there was never any bad blood between them.

Henry was still dogged by bouts of severe colds and influenza and was not nearly fit enough for the rigours of early naval life at Osborne and Dartmouth.

37. Princes Henry and Albert on their bicycles with Princess Mary, 1912. The court was in mourning for the death of their uncle, King Frederick VIII of Denmark, hence the black dress and arm-bands.

Instead, his housemaster at St Peter's Court suggested that he should go to Eton. He thought Mr Lubbock's house would suit him best, particularly for entry into the Army class. From the earliest age, King George V had instilled into his children a sense of the wonders of the Royal Navy. All of his sons wanted to follow him into the Senior Service, except for Henry, who had always wanted to be a soldier.

While working for the entrance exams for Eton, both Henry and George went down with what the doctors thought was whooping cough and it was thought better that they did not return home for the Easter holidays of 1913. Hansell was

38. The Prince of Wales (left) in his Knight of the Garter Robes, with Princes George and Henry, in Highland dress, with their sister, Princess Mary, and Prince Albert in the uniform of a Naval Cadet before the Coronation of their father as King George V in 1911.

detailed to take them both to Cornwall and the King wrote, 'You can play golf and sit around in the sun . . . it is a beautiful climate.' His assessment was wildly out and Hansell likened the weather to a cross between the South of France and the North Pole. Henry ran a temperature of 100° and the local doctor diagnosed bronchial pneumonia. When he recovered, he returned to St Peter's Court for his last term where he sat and easily passed the exam to Eton, gaining a place in the middle fourth—one form up from the bottom. His headmaster was sorry to see him go, writing, 'I have really got to like him very much. He has developed so much in seriousness & thoughtfulness without losing any of his love of fun . . . everybody liked him.'

George missed his companion brother at St Peter's Court. Like the rest of his family, he was totally unpretentious and his natural charm made him popular amongst the boys and the staff. George reverted to the schooling of his eldest brothers and went to Osborne in 1916. As a child at York Cottage he had told his father that he had made up his mind to enter the Royal Navy.

'Splendid,' his father replied. 'I suppose you want to be a sailor because I am one?'
'No-o,' he replied cautiously. 'I don't like lessons, and it doesn't take much brains
to be a sailor, does it?'

The youngest child, John, spent much of his short life away from his family.
Initially, he was brought up in exactly the same way as his elder brothers, but it
soon became apparent that he was an epileptic and his doctors thought that his
presence would be unsettling in the schoolroom. So from the age of twelve, he
lived completely apart from his family under the care of 'Lalla', his nanny, and a
male servant. He was a friendly, outgoing little boy, a favourite with his brothers
and sister, but he died quite suddenly on 18 January 1919 at the age of thirteen
at Wood Farm on the Sandringham estate. Queen Mary wrote in her diary: 'The
news gave me a great shock, tho' for the poor little boy's restless soul, death came
as a great release.' He was buried in the churchyard at Sandringham, and among
the tributes was a wreath of flowers from Queen Alexandra with a card, 'To
darling, darling Johnnie, from his broken-hearted old Grannie.'

Shortly after John died, King George V wrote to his secretary and confidant,
Lord Stamfordham: 'Yes, my sons have begun well, especially the eldest, who
has become most popular & has already made a name for himself. They will be of
great assistance to me in the future.' Although David, his heir, was later to
become a disappointment to him, he was able to rely on his other sons and
daughter to perform their official duties. His attitude towards them had altered
little since their childhoods. He chaffed them for their conduct, their clothes and
their friends and what he considered the slackness of the post-war age. His
pragmatic criticism was taken badly and with resentment. However, this
disapproval ceased when each of his children married, Bertie to Lady Elizabeth
Bowes-Lyon, Mary to Viscount Lascelles, heir to the Earl of Harewood, Henry to
Lady Alice Montagu-Douglas-Scott and George to Princess Marina of Greece—
David did not marry in his father's lifetime and never experienced his father's
amelioration. For the rest of the King's life, his married children were to enjoy
the warmth and genial affection that each had enjoyed in the early part of their
childhood.

3

Queen Elizabeth, the Queen Mother

In a television interview at the time of Queen Elizabeth, the Queen Mother's eightieth birthday, the Prince of Wales confided:

> Ever since I can remember, my Grandmother has been the most wonderful example of fun, laughter, warmth, infinite security and, above all else, exquisite taste in all things. For me, she will always be one of those extraordinary, rare people whose touch can turn everything to gold—whether it be putting people at their ease, turning something dull into something amusing, bringing happiness and comfort to people, or making any house she lives in a unique haven of cosiness and character.

The Queen Mother would surely be the first to agree that those very qualities stem from her enchanted childhood and the influence of her loving parents.

On 4 August 1900, the Honourable Elizabeth Angela Marguerite Bowes-Lyon was born at St Paul's Walden Bury, the Hertfordshire home of her parents, Lord and Lady Glamis. At her baptism in the local parish church of All Saints on 23 September, she was christened Elizabeth—a family name since the fourteenth century when Sir John Lyon married Jean, the daughter of Robert II and Elizabeth of Scotland—and Marguerite after the sister of the first Duke of Portland, a Cavendish-Bentinck ancestress of her mother.

The Bowes-Lyon children thought of themselves more as a 'clan' than a family for there were already seven of them in the nursery by the time Elizabeth was born. The eldest was Mary, almost seventeen, the youngest Michael, approaching seven. Between those two were Patrick (the Master of Glamis), John, Alexander, Fergus and Rose. An elder child, Violet Hyacinth, had died seven years earlier of diphtheria.

Born at the end of Queen Victoria's reign, Elizabeth was fortunate in her Victorian, but liberal, parents. Lady Glamis was a remarkable woman. She took an active part in raising her children—an unusual step in her day—and it was her very presence, and her charm and sympathy rather than any harsh treatment, that controlled her large 'brood'. Gifted in music and artistic subjects like needlework and painting, she was also an exceptionally fine and creative

39. Part of the grounds of St Paul's Walden Bury, Hertfordshire, the birthplace and childhood home of Elizabeth Bowes-Lyon.

gardener. Lord Glamis, formerly a lieutenant in the Life Guards, was tall and erect with a large moustache. He had left the army as soon as his father granted him the St Paul's Walden Bury estate between Hitchin and Welwyn. A great countryman with an expert knowledge of estate management, he cared deeply for his tenantry and for the welfare of his staff. Above all, he possessed a quiet dignity and a mild manner coupled with a deep sense of duty. These characteristics and accomplishments of both parents were passed on to all of their children and especially to Elizabeth.

As a baby, Elizabeth was forward and enterprising, crawling and talking early and walking soon after her first birthday. In a letter to a friend, Lady Glamis wrote that, 'Elizabeth is learning to walk—very dangerous!' When she was a few weeks old a nurse, Clara Cooper Knight, affectionately known as 'Alla', was engaged and stayed with the family for another eleven years—the same 'Alla' would, fifteen years later, care for the next generation of royal children, the Princesses Elizabeth and Margaret Rose. The youngest child, particularly when a girl, is always spoilt in a large family, but in Elizabeth's case the spoiling had no

40. 'Princess', otherwise Elizabeth Bowes-Lyon, on her second birthday at St Paul's Walden Bury.

detrimental effect and indeed, only enhanced her natural charm. She was not the youngest for long, for her 'darling bruvver', David, was born early in 1902. Quite soon Elizabeth and her brother were known by the family as 'the Benjamins,' an Old Testament analogy to Benjamin, the youngest, and favourite, of Jacob's sons, and, being the nearest in age, a close bond of affection grew between them that was to last all their lives.

Lord Glamis succeeded to the title of the Earl of Strathmore and Kinghorne on the death of his father in 1904 and his youngest daughter became The Lady Elizabeth Bowes-Lyon, not that this title meant much to the four-year-old child.

In addition to St Paul's Walden Bury, Lord Strathmore inherited Glamis Castle in Scotland, the domain of the Lyon family for over 600 years and Streatlam Castle in Durham, the former seat of the Bowes family.

The Strathmores were immensely grand, 'so grand that you didn't notice that they were grand at all'. Like royalty, they had several houses which they visited at set periods of the year with their servants. August and September every year were spent at Glamis Castle in Tayside and Elizabeth was there for her first birthday. Where St Paul's Walden Bury was enchanting, Glamis had a special brand of magic and romanticism that fired Elizabeth's fertile and imaginative young mind. The castle, with deep red sandstone walls and tall turrets like a French château, was as solid as the neighbouring Grampian mountains and steeped in legend and family history. The other family house, Streatlam Castle in Durham, did not feature for long in Elizabeth's life, for it was soon sold to pay off death duties and later pulled down.

Although the Strathmores had taken 20 St James's Square in London as their 'town' house, where they stayed during the season, home to Elizabeth and her family was undoubtedly St Paul's Walden Bury. The house, gardens and estate

41. The Strathmore family. From left to right, Fergus, John, Lord Strathmore, Mary, Patrick and Alexander; seated are Rose, Lady Strathmore, holding the youngest, David, with Elizabeth and Michael.

were all any child could wish for. 'The Bury', as the Queen Anne house is known locally, is large and rambling, and looks as if several houses have been pushed together. It is nonetheless a pretty house with magnolia and sweet-scented honeysuckle flowering in summer against weathered red-brick walls. The childrens' 'territory', the day and night nurseries, were in the west wing. They were typical of the age, large and plain. The day nursery had heavy well-worn furniture, and a high brass fender guarded the open log fire. A Victorian screen, with a bright collage of cut-outs, stood in the corner and favourite illustrations from picture books, framed by the estate carpenter, hung on the walls. In the cupboards were a host of toys, again rather worn, having been passed down from brother to sister.

The gardens, said to have been laid out by Le Nôtre of Versailles fame, were full of excitement to a child. The 'Benjamins' would explore the 'cloisters'—the grassy rides cut through woods of oak and beech, silver birch and firs that radiated out from the house and gave an impression of immense size. The statues, rock garden, croquet lawn and tennis court and the lake with its islands and punt were a source of constant interest and amusement to them. It was recalled by Elizabeth, writing in the third person, shortly before her wedding:

> At the bottom of the garden, where the sun always seems to be shining, in THE WOOD—the haunt of fairies, with its anemonies and ponds, and moss grown statues, and the BIG OAK under which she reads and where ring doves, Caroline-Curly-Love and Rhoda-Wrigly-Worm, contentedly coo in their wicker-work 'Ideal Home'.
>
> There are carpets of primroses and anemonies to sit on and she generally has tea either in the shadow of the statue of Diana or near another very favourite one called the 'Running Footman' or the 'Bounding Butler' (to grown-up people known as the Discus-Thrower). These statues live in cut-out grassy places, and sometimes there are wild strawberries around them, sometimes bee-orchises.

The 'Benjamins' had their own garden, an unkempt affair with a small pond. Elizabeth inherited her mother's flair for gardening and knew all the plants and trees by name; some were even given names made up by the 'Benjamins'. Best of all for them, were the out-buildings. While the harness room and the stables were 'attractive', 'nothing was quite so good as the Flea House'—the still room in the attic of a tumbledown brewhouse. It was their 'lair', the centre of their fantasy world, reached only by a rickety ladder and inaccessible to 'grown-ups'. There they kept a store of fruit and sweets, biscuits filched from the kitchens and, later, packets of 'Woodies' (Woodbine cigarettes) and matches.

Animals, too, played a major part in Lady Elizabeth's early life. The hens and the bantams ('whose-eggs-are-so-good-for-tea') who lived in the Flea House had to be fed and cared for. There was a tame bulfinch called Bobby who flew into the day nursery, strutting up and down the table, helping himself to food off their plates. One day a cat killed Bobby and David's cedar pencil box, lined with rose petals, was made into a coffin for the bird. Bobby was then buried in a deep grave in their garden to a long funeral oration intoned by Elizabeth.

42. Lady Elizabeth Bowes-Lyon at the age of nine on her pony, 'Bobs', in the garden at St Paul's Walden Bury.

At the 'Bury' there was the usual assortment of dogs to be found in any country house—the shooting dogs of her father and brothers, her mother's lap dog and her own. There were other animals, too, in Elizabeth's life, like the tortoises, the Persian cats with their kittens, and the goats and horses. One pony, Bobs, was a special favourite. The love lavished on this fat little Shetland was reciprocated and it followed its young mistress around the garden like a dog, walking up and down steps and into the house if given the chance. The housekeeper, Mrs Thompson, remembers Elizabeth coming up to the window of her sitting room with ' . . . her pony Bobs, and making him beg for sugar'. Elizabeth rode well and her love of horses, on and off the race course, has remained with her ever since.

Among the other favourites were two pure black Berkshire pigs called Lucifer and Emma. Every day the 'Benjamins' would go to the sty, feed the pigs with windfall apples and scratch their fat backs and stub noses. One day they arrived at the sty to find that Lucifer was missing. To their horror, they learned that he had been given to the Church fête as the prize for the raffle. Miserable, they

109

43. The ninth birthday portrait of Lady Elizabeth Bowes-Lyon.

raided their money boxes and sought loans from family and staff but they raised only enough to corner half the tickets sold—even money on Lucifer's safe return. Luck was not with them and Lucifer was lost forever.

People, too, fell under the spell of the young Elizabeth, for she enchanted almost every one she met. Even at the age of three, when she was so small that she could only climb the stairs one at a time, she would show visitors to the Bury to their rooms. Once, when the land agent came to the house, Elizabeth greeted him: 'How do you do, Mr Ralston. I haven't seen you look so well, not for years and years! But I am sure you will be sorry to learn that Lord Strathmore has got the toothache.' From the very beginning, Elizabeth had that knack of making everyone feel at ease, whatever their age or background. When conversation grew sticky with some guest, the cry would go up, 'Where's Elizabeth?' When she arrived, the guest would be charmed by the small child with violet-blue eyes and a cascade of black curls and the opening conversation gambit, 'Shall us talk now?' Should some visitor call at the house without warning, Elizabeth, at a very early age, would order and serve tea in her mother's absence. One such guest, Lord Gorell, wrote of her after his visit:

> To every lover of children she had about her that indefinable charm that bears elders into fairyland. In the simplest and most unconscious way she was all-conquering. In addition to the charm of especially winsome childhood, she had, even then, that blend of kindliness and dignity that is the peculiar characteristic of her family. She was small for her age, responsive as a harp, wistful and appealing one moment, bright-eyed and eager the next, with a flashing smile of appreciative delight, an elfin creature swift of movement . . . quick of intelligence, alive with humour, able to join in any of the jokes, and touchingly and sometimes amusingly loyal to her friends.

Her natural talent to bring people out was not confined to the 'grown-ups'. Scores of boys fell for Elizabeth. After Christmas the family would always stay at their house in St James's Square, going to the pantomime at Drury Lane Theatre or to the many parties to which the children were invited. At one such party, given by the Countess of Leicester, Elizabeth met a shy boy called Bertie when she was five. The story goes that she charmed this ten-year-old and gave him the cherries off the top of her cake. He never forgot their meeting. Another childhood contemporary was Lord David Cecil who was one of her playmates in Hyde Park in London. He later recalled her 'sweetness and sense of fun; and a certain roguish quality. The personality I see now was there already.' One recalls the very similar assessment expressed by the Prince of Wales to the press on first meeting Lady Diana Spencer.

It was, perhaps, these qualities that her family and friends saw in Elizabeth from the start that earned her the nickname, with remarkable prophecy, of 'Princess'. She certainly looked the part as she dressed up in early seventeenth-century dresses and her family would play up to her as they knelt and kissed her outstretched hand.

44. 'The Benjamins'—Lady Elizabeth and David Bowes-Lyon—wearing clothes from the 'dressing-up box'.

45. Lady Elizabeth Bowes-Lyon, right, with a guest at Glamis *c.* 1911.

For the 'Benjamins', life at the Bury was not all play and perpetual holiday. Lady Strathmore began their education early, teaching them to read herself. Elizabeth was an avid pupil and learnt quickly. She loved to hear her mother read Bible stories and then to read them for herself. History was another great love and it had an added interest for her because her ancestors were an integral part of Scottish history. A direct descendant of Robert the Bruce, her forebears included a Lord Glamis who was slain at Flodden in 1513, another who died in the Battle of Sherriffmuir in 1715, others who were killed in various clan skirmishes with their neighbours the Crawfords, and one Lady Glamis who was burned as a witch in Edinburgh in 1537.

46. Glamis Castle, seat of the Lyon family since the fourteenth century.

Music and drawing were also part of their schoolroom activities, as well as dancing, which was taught both at home and in nearby Hitchin at private lessons at the Sun Hotel. At a very early age the 'Benjamins', in particular Elizabeth, were entertaining their parents and their guests with some pretty little dances. Their skill at dancing and their interest in history fitted in well with their love of dressing-up. There were dozens of clothes, some centuries old, in the dressing-up box. They would perform a play or dance as much for their own pleasure as for the family audience.

The young Elizabeth Bowes-Lyon and her home life sound too good to be true, but, as with any large family, there are always disagreements and arguments. Tremendous fights would break out in the nursery over some trivial matter and the two youngest, as always, would team up together until the danger passed. Once, at the age of six and for no apparent reason, Elizabeth cut up a pair of new sheets. She owned up to her mother who, as always, reproved her by simply saying *Elizabeth!* in a sad voice. It was hardly considered a vice but Elizabeth had a passion for chocolate cake and cream biscuits. The housekeeper, Mrs Thompson, indulged this sweet tooth and remembers her '. . . tripping lightly down the stairs and it would be 'Mrs Thompson, have you any of those nice creams left for us?' and she would herself open the cupboard and help herself to what she liked best.' The cook was not so benevolent. 'The little imp', she wrote, 'I was forever chasing her out my kitchen.'

Practical jokes were a constant source of amusement. Once, the 'Benjamins' wedged an inflated football bladder under the front wheel of their parents' car. The Strathmores sat in the back and the chauffeur—a former coachman and totally unmechanical—drove off. The resultant bang from beneath the bonnet caused tremendous alarm, much to the glee of the hidden duo. Another source of amusement was to tell the guests at Glamis of the ghosts that haunted the castle. Elizabeth would relate stories of Old Beardy, the ghost of Earl Beardie who walked the corridors at night, or the Grey Lady who is a sign of good luck. Then the 'Benjamins' would dress up a dummy from the acting-box and leave it strategically placed by a doorway to one of the romantically-named rooms, the King Malcolm's room, the Prince Charlie room or Hangman's room. The results, alas, are not recorded.

It was a bitter blow when David, went away to school in 1912. Elizabeth wrote to a friend from Glamis, 'David went to school for the first time on Friday last. I believe he is quite enjoying it. I miss him horribly . . .' She stayed at home having her own lessons in the schoolroom under a succession of governesses. Most were French and Elizabeth spoke their language well by the age of ten. Governesses varied in their appeal to her. One was summed up by her pupil in the opening line of an essay on 'The Sea': 'Some governesses are nice and some are not.' A girls' day school in London was tried for two terms but it was not a success although she did win an essay prize. After that, it was back to the schoolroom at the Bury. Piano and dancing lessons, however, continued at her music school in London where she excelled in both, and after only six months' tuition she was picked to give the star performance at the end of the school's concert.

During the Easter holidays, Elizabeth and David were taught German by a charming governess, Fraulein Kathie Keubler. Before she returned to Germany, she left behind an observation of her charge: 'she had a small delicate figure, a sensitive, somewhat pale little face, dark hair and very beautiful violet blue eyes . . . far more mature and understanding than her years warranted.' Fraulein Keubler was replaced by an English governess who coached Elizabeth for her Junior Oxford examinations, which she passed at well below the average age.

Life for Elizabeth continued in much the same vein—lessons in the schoolroom at the Bury, visits to their London house for music and dancing lessons and then the late summer spent at Glamis where the whole family would congregate from school or university, the older married brothers and sister with their spouses and children. With a few guests to make up the numbers, the family could even raise a cricket team and much of their time was spent challenging other house parties in the area.

The treat for Elizabeth's fourteenth birthday was to see a variety show at the London Coliseum. At the end of one particular performance in 1914 there was an announcement that ' . . . His Majesty's Government had accordingly notified the German Government that a state of war exists between the two countries as from 11 pm today.' As she sat in the box, surrounded by her family, she witnessed the wild excitement and patriotric fervour that followed the news.

The declaration of war had an immediate effect on Elizabeth. Her four brothers went to join up in the army, three to their local Scottish regiment, the Black Watch, and one to the Royal Scots (Alexander, the third brother, had died three years before). Her unmarried sister, Rose, went to train as a nurse and plans were put into operation to turn part of Glamis into a convalescent home for the wounded. Within a week, Elizabeth and her mother were at Glamis helping with the preparations. Much later, she remembered that time as 'the bustle of hurried visits to the chemists for outfits of every sort of medicine and to the gunsmith's to buy all those things that people thought they wanted for a war and then found they didn't.' It was a time of furious 'knitting, knitting and knitting', and crumpling up tissue paper until it was soft enough to stuff into sleeping bags.

The first of the wounded arrived at Glamis in December 1914 and Elizabeth was with her mother at the front door to welcome them as if they were staying for a house party. Sixteen beds had been arranged in the dining-room and the men were allowed to use the billiard-room for recreation and to eat in the crypt. Rose returned to take charge of the wounded but Elizabeth was thought too young and inexperienced for actual nursing. Nevertheless, there was plenty to keep her occupied. She fetched and carried, wrote letters for those who could not write, played whist and generally made the inmates feel at home. She would entertain them by playing the piano and singing the popular songs of the day. They in turn adored her for her care and concern. One corporal wrote of her, 'She had the loveliest pair of blue eyes I've ever seen—expressive, eloquent eyes that could speak for themselves. She had a very taking habit of knitting her forehead just a little now and then when she was speaking, and her smile was a refreshment.'

This new life with increased responsibilities did nothing to dampen the spirit of the 'Benjamins'. One holiday, Elizabeth dressed up her brother David as a very grand maiden aunt. She led this heavily made-up, elderly 'woman', with a large hat, veil and long skirt, into the ward and with a respectful tone introduced each soldier. David asked all the right questions and received deferential replies. The next day, when the joke was revealed, the language of the inmates was far from suitable for a maiden aunt.

Tragedy stuck the Strathmore family when Fergus was killed at the Battle of Loos in September 1915. He had just returned to the front from leave spent at Glamis where he had been staying for the birth of his first child, Rosemary Lusia. Lady Strathmore felt the loss deeply and her health began to suffer. Consequently, more and more of her mother's role of running the castle and family fell onto Elizabeth's young shoulders and when her sister Rose left to marry in May 1916, the responsibilities of the sickroom were added to her burden. She coped, as usual, with ability far beyond her years. From then on, she could no longer be considered a teenage girl but a woman.

Just before Christmas 1916, Elizabeth spotted smoke billowing from the top of the ninety-foot tower. She ran to telephone the fire brigade, not only the local ones in Forfar and Glamis but also the larger brigade at Dundee. Her foresight

47. Lady Elizabeth Bowes-Lyon, with her warm smile, welcomes one of the first casualties of the First World War to Glamis Castle, watched by her sister, Lady Rose Leveson-Gower, 1915.

48. Lady Strathmore, seated on the wicker chair in the front, surrounded by the convalescents at Glamis Castle. Lady Elizabeth Bowes-Lyon is seated on her right.

undoubtedly saved the castle, for when the local fire engines arrived their hoses were not long enough to pump water from the River Dean a few hundred yards away. The Dundee fire engines eventually managed to quell the blaze. In the meantime, the intense heat had melted a large lead tank in the roof and the water came cascading down the spiral staircase. Elizabeth organised every available hand to sweep the water away from the drawing-room and other apartments with all their treasures and then to set up a human chain to take the pictures and rugs out on to the lawn. It took nearly ten years to restore that part of the castle.

The war dragged on for another two years and it was not until the summer of 1919 that the last of the wounded left Glamis, nearly five years since the first arrivals. In peacetime, a girl of Elizabeth's standing would have enjoyed her youth, completed her education at some finishing school, possibly abroad, and then been launched into society. All that was denied to her. Instead, by witnessing at first hand suffering and family tragedy, she had gained experience and maturity. She had displayed tact, natural charm and compassion for others and shown her ability for hard work and courage.

During the London summer season of 1920, Elizabeth met Bertie, then Duke of York, at a ball. They met again at Glamis a few months later where the shy, stammering Bertie began to realise that he was in love with her. Elizabeth was certainly not in love with him and she was far too busy with her family, enjoying herself and entertaining their large house parties to take much notice of him. The next year, Bertie summoned up enough courage to propose to Elizabeth. The fact that she turned him down did nothing to dampen his resolve, nor did his father's discouraging remark before the proposal, 'You'll be lucky if you get her'.

Bertie continued to see Elizabeth as often as possible, contriving to be asked to the same parties or staying at either of the Strathmore country houses. Bertie, however, was not her only suitor and five eligible men proposed to her during 1922, all of whom she turned down. By the time Bertie arrived at St Paul's Walden Bury on 13 January 1923, Elizabeth knew him better, and understood and admired him more than the time when he had proposed eighteen months before. Instead of joining the rest of the family at church one Sunday morning, Bertie took Elizabeth off for a walk in the woods she had loved as a child. There, he proposed to her again and this time, to his great joy, she finally accepted him.

Elizabeth was amazed at her own decision to become a royal duchess and initially dismayed at taking on the daunting role ahead of her—a case, perhaps, of her head ruling her heart. But, since her background, her nature and her forceful character had already equipped her for the task, she soon realised that her impulsive decision was the right one. The family nickname of her childhood, 'Princess', finally came true.

4

Elizabeth and Margaret – the Little Princesses

It is one of those strange anomalies of Royal life that, for the first three years of their marriage, the Duke and Duchess of York, later to become King George VI and Queen Elizabeth, had no permanent home of their own. They began their married life at White Lodge in Richmond Park but they found it too far from the capital to use as a London house and, thereafter, the Duke and Duchess lived with relations 'out of a suitcase' or in rented houses.

At the beginning of 1926, for no apparent reason, various magazines began to carry articles and photographs of the Duke and Duchess of York. Unlike today, there was no announcement from Buckingham Palace as to why the popular Duchess was not now seen in public so often, but the two facts were connected and it was surmised that she was pregnant. The homeless Duke then rented another house in London, 40 Grovesnor Square. The Duchess had already decided that she did not want her baby born in 'rented accomodation' but at her father's London house, 17 Bruton Street. This was an imposing residence between Berkeley Square and Bond Street, in the heart of fashionable Mayfair. After spending Christmas at Sandringham, the Duke and Duchess moved there in January 1926,

On the evening of 20 April, the house in Bruton Street was milling with people. With the Duchess in her bedroom on the first floor was the leading obstetric surgeon of the day, Sir Henry Simson, assisted by Sir George Blacker, Walter Jagger and Mrs Clara Knight, the faithful 'Alla' of the Duchess's own nursery days. Below, the Duke waited with her parents, the Earl and Countess of Strathmore, and the Home Secretary, Sir William Joynson-Hicks, whose constitutional presence was still obligatory at royal births. In the early hours of the next morning, it was he who announced that 'Her Royal Highness, the Duchess of York, was safely delivered of a Princess at 2.40 am this morning, Wednesday, April 21st. Her Royal Highness and the infant Princess are making very satisfactory progress'. The surgeons, in their statement added that 'a certain line of treatment was successfully adopted'. The Princess Elizabeth of York was, in fact, born by Caesarean section.

The duty equerry at Windsor Castle, Captain Reginald Seymour, wakened the

13. Princesses Elizabeth and Margaret in the gardens of Windsor Castle, 1941.

14. Princess Anne as a Brownie of the '1st B'ham Palace' Pack, aged nine, in 1959.

15. Princess Anne at a gymkhana at Ascot, April 1963.

16. The Queen Mother holding Prince Andrew, with Prince Charles and Princess Anne, on her sixtieth birthday, August 1960.

17. Cecil Beaton's photograph of Prince Andrew in the Music Room of Buckingham Palace, 1963.

49. The day nursery at 145 Piccadilly, the first London home of the Duke and Duchess of York (later King George VI and Queen Elizabeth). Much of the nursery furniture was taken to Buckingham Palace and Clarence House for subsequent generations of royal children.

King and Queen at 4 o'clock and told them the news 'that darling Elizabeth had got a daughter . . . Such a relief and joy', as Queen Mary later wrote in her diary.

From her bedroom, the Duchess of York could hear the twenty-one gun salute fired in Hyde Park, followed by another at the Tower of London in honour of the birth of her daughter. Then the family visitors began to arrive. Princess Mary was the first and received a cheer from the crowd of several hundred that had gathered outside, despite the weather that had 'been evil for a week'. In the afternoon, the King and Queen motored up from Windsor and were thrilled with their first granddaughter, ' . . . a little darling with a lovely complexion with fair hair', although Queen Mary wished the baby was more like her mother.

The Countess of Airlie, a lady-in-waiting to Queen Mary, was one of the first outside the family to visit the Duchess. She wrote, 'I little thought then that I was paying homage to the future Queen of England, for in those days there was every expectation that the Prince of Wales would marry within the next year or two'. It was a common view, because it was quite likely that the Duke and Duchess of York would have more children, among them, maybe, a son, and, more likely, that his brother, the Prince of Wales would produce his own heir to the throne.

While the crowds waited in Bruton Street and the medical bulletins reported 'satisfactory progress', the Duke of York wrote to his mother,

> You don't know what a tremendous joy it is to Elizabeth and me to have our little girl. We always wanted a child to make our happiness complete, & now that it had at last happened, it seems so wonderful & strange. I am so proud of Elizabeth at this moment after all she has gone through during the last few days . . . I do hope that you & Papa are as delighted as we are, to have a granddaughter . . . May I say I hope you won't spoil her when she gets a bit older.

The christening was held in the chapel at Buckingham Palace on 29 May, two weeks after the collapse of the General Strike. The traditional trappings for royal christenings, the gold lily font and the Honiton lace robes, were brought up from Windsor and the font was filled with water from the River Jordan. The Duke and Duchess chose the names Elizabeth Alexandra Mary—'We are so anxious', wrote the Duke to his father, 'for her first name to be Elizabeth as it is such a nice name & there has been no one of that name in your family for such a long time. Elizabeth of York sounds nice too.' His father agreed and approved the choice of the other names, those of his mother and wife, but, after some reflection, thought

50. Princess Elizabeth with her nanny, Clara Knight ('Alla'), being driven up the Mall, London, aged two.

it unnecessary to include Victoria as the Princess was so unlikely to accede to the Throne.

The Archbishop of York, Dr Cosmo Laing, performed the ceremony and six members of the family stood as sponsors—royal godparents. They were the grandparents, the King, Queen and the Earl of Strathmore, an aunt from each side of the family—Princess Mary and Lady Elphinstone—and, a venerable link with the past, Queen Victoria's third son, the Duke of Connaught. The baby cried throughout the ceremony and Alla resorted to an old-fashioned remedy of dosing her with dill water, much to the surprise of the women present and the amusement of the Prince of Wales. Surprisingly, only a few newspapers carried an account of the christening or published the photograph of the simple cake decorated with the white roses of the House of York and a little silver cradle with a baby inside.

Such was the initial interest in the latest royal baby that Alla had to smuggle Elizabeth out of the back door of Bruton Street when she went for her 'airing'. But soon the interest began to wane and Alla could push her in her pram up to the gravel paths of Berkeley Square or down to Green Park unnoticed—only those with sharp eyes would have recognised the crest on the side of the pram. The York household soon settled into that regular routine so beloved by nannies, and Alla, assisted by a nursery maid, Margaret MacDonald, looked after Elizabeth completely. They fed, bathed, dressed and exercised her twice a day, and at tea time, brought her down to her parents in a clean dress.

In August, when Elizabeth was five months old, the Duke and Duchess of York left Bruton Street to stay at another Strathmore house, Glamis Castle in Scotland. These summer visits to Glamis were to become a regular and enjoyable feature of Elizabeth's childhood. For the rest of that summer, Elizabeth spent much of her time either asleep in her pram in the beautiful garden created by Lady Strathmore, or in the nursery, or with her grandmother, while her parents visited friends.

Back in London, the Duke and Duchess were busy with the preparations for their six-month tour of New Zealand and Australia in the New Year. In addition to their heavy round of commitments, they had to plan their new home, for the Duke had signed the lease on 145 Piccadilly, a large but dilapidated Adam-style house at Hyde Park Corner, which they hoped to move into on their return from their Commonwealth Tour.

Despite these pressures, the Duchess found the time to play with her baby. A contemporary account shows her kneeling on the floor in front of Elizabeth, aged six months, sitting on a sofa:

No doubt about it, a Princess. She was sitting up by herself in the middle of a huge chesterfield, like a white fluff of thistledown. Her hair is very fair and beginning to curl charmingly—owing, the Duchess says, to the untiring attention of her nurse. The baby is always good, she has the sweetest air of complete serenity.

The York family had Christmas together and the Duchess gave Elizabeth a coral necklace. Their sad parting came at Victoria Station on 6 January 1927 and the Duchess later wrote to Queen Mary, 'I felt very much leaving on Thursday, and the baby was so sweet playing with the buttons on Bertie's uniform that it quite broke me up.' Queen Mary must certainly have symphathised, for she herself, twenty-five years before, had made the same tour, leaving her young family behind.

Both sets of grandparents had agreed to care for Elizabeth. She went first to St Paul's Walden Bury, the Hertfordshire home of the Strathmores, where she slept in the same night nursery, played with the same toys and was looked after by the same woman as her mother, a quarter of a century before. Also like her mother, Elizabeth loved dogs and spent hours with the Countess's two chows, Brownie and Blackie, burying her tiny fists in their soft fur.

In February, Elizabeth went to stay with 'Grandpapa England' and Queen Mary at Buckingham Palace. They were devoted to her and, having mellowed in old age, gave her the love that they had been incapable of showing to their own children. They spoilt her dreadfully and greatly looked forward to playing with her when Alla brought her down to tea every afternoon.

The King sent news of Elizabeth to her parents and in March wrote, 'Your sweet little daughter . . . is growing daily. She has four teeth now, which is quite good at eleven months old, she is very happy . . .' The Duke, remembering the wonderful times he had had with his grandfather during his parents' tour, replied that he hoped that she was not being spoilt. If she was being spoilt, it was rather by her own parents, for every stop on their high-successful tour produced another crop of toys for the baby. Three tons of toys were brought back and later distributed amongst the needy children of Durham.

The Duke and Duchess of York returned to London on 27 June 1927 and were reunited with their fourteen-month-old baby at Buckingham Palace. The crowd surged towards the railings for their balcony appearance and an ecstatic cheer went up when Elizabeth was brought out with the King and Queen. There was a second balcony appearance that day when the Duke and Duchess moved to their new home, 145 Piccadilly. A Persian rug was draped over the balustrade and the Duchess carried Elizabeth out to the prolonged applause of the crowd below.

145 Piccadilly suited the Duke and Duchess well. In their absence it had been modernised to a high standard and the decoration and furnishings reflected the Duchess's excellent taste and her great flair, inherited from her mother, for making a comfortable home. The top floor of the house was devoted to the nurseries. Among the heavy, mahogany furniture were a grandfather clock, a glass-fronted display cabinet for the more delicate toys and a rocking chair for Alla. One of the main advantages of the house for Elizabeth was that it backed on to Hamilton Gardens, a private garden with a small lake, with the open spaces of Hyde Park beyond.

There was much of her mother as a child in the young Elizabeth. From an early age she greeted the visitors who came to the house and developed an instant rapport with them. One guest remembers her in the nursery standing 'so sweetly and without the slightest shyness, waiting to be kissed'. She also enjoyed meeting people whenever she went with her parents to stay with their relations at Balmoral, Glamis, St Paul's Walden Bury or at Naseby Hall in Northamptonshire, the house the Duke took during the winter of 1928 to hunt with the Pytchley Hounds.

Naseby was a happy place for the York family. The Duke enjoyed hunting and it was there that Elizabeth first sat on a horse—she was given a pony as a Christmas present the following year and soon learnt to ride well, much to the approval of her grandfather. These country pursuits were soon checked, however, as word reached them that the King, who had caught a chill at the Armistice Day ceremonies, had bronchial pneumonia. His condition worsened and the Christmas visit to Sandringham was cancelled. The whole family remained in London and Elizabeth was allowed to stay up late and listen to the carol singers on Christmas Eve. When she heard the lines in 'Hark the herald angel sing',

> Glad tidings of great joy I bring
> To you and all mankind,

she shrieked with glee, 'I know who Old Man Kind is!'— her grandfather.

'Grandpapa England' nearly died during those winter months and only his strong will pulled him through his many operations and relapses. His doctors decided that he should go to the South Coast, and a house near Bognor, 'Craigweil', was chosen for his convalescence. The King was joined by Elizabeth and Alla in March 1929, shortly before her third birthday. She was a boon companion and the King was delighted to see her. She played in the garden and made sandcastles in the sandpit the King had provided for her. When he recovered enough to go outside, he took Elizabeth's hand and walked along the sea front, where they acknowledged the cheers of the crowd, he with a slight nod of the head, Elizabeth waving warmly.

King George so enjoyed Elizabeth's bright company that when he returned to Buckingham Palace he arranged to see her every morning. She would go to an upstairs window of 145 Piccadilly just after breakfast and wave to her grandfather across Green Park and Constitution Hill.

There seemed nothing to cloud the happy atmosphere and established routine of 145 Piccadilly and Elizabeth thrived on the love and affection of her family. She was an obedient and obliging child and responded to their attentions of the nursery staff. Since she had first started to talk, Elizabeth had been called 'Lilibet' from the time when she attempted her own name and it came out as 'Lilliebeth', and the name has stuck with members of her family to this day. Unwittingly, Elizabeth was becoming a cult figure. Her photographs were seen everywhere, in newspapers and on chocolate boxes. When it was seen that her clothes were predominately yellow, manufacturers catered for the rush demand for children's clothes in that colour.

In May 1929, the Duke of York was created Lord High Commissioner. This ecclesiastical appointment meant that the Duke and Duchess had to spend the summer at the Palace of Holyrood House. When Elizabeth was left behind in London, her mother wrote, 'I fear that it has been a very great disappointment to the people [the Scots], not that they would have seen her, but they would have liked to feel that she was here . . . it almost frightens me that the people should love her so much. I suppose that it is a good thing, and I hope that she will be worthy of it, poor little darling'.

If the Scots were upset that Elizabeth had not gone to Edinburgh, at least they were compensated by the birth of Margaret Rose, the Duke and Duchess of York's second child, at Glamis in 1930. Fearing a difficult birth, the same gathering of doctors and surgeons had assembled at the castle including the Home Secretary, this time Joseph Clynes in Ramsay MacDonald's Labour Cabinet. They all had a long wait. Most of the party had arrived for the Duchess's birthday on 4 August but after several false alarms, the baby was not born until the evening of 21 August. She weighed six pounds eleven ounces.

The Home Secretary went down to the music-room where 'the Duke of York, the child's grandmother, another doctor, nurses and a few privileged persons were waiting' and saw not the Prince that everyone was so confidently expecting, but another girl. Clynes's assistant sent off the usual telegram: 'Yesterday evening at 22 minutes after nine o'clock Her Royal Highness the Duchess of York was safely delivered of a Princess at Glamis Castle . . .' The three doctors, all Scotsmen, added that 'Her Royal Highness and the infant Princess are doing fine'. The Scots term 'doing fine' was amended for the English announcement to 'doing well'.

The birth was received warmly throughout the country. Bells pealed, flags and bunting fluttered in the wet weather and the traditional gun salutes boomed in Hyde Park and the Tower of London. A great brushwood fire was lit on the top of Hunter's Hill on the Glamis estate and the skirl of Glamis pipe band floated over the moors in honour of the new Princess.

It was no secret that the Duke and Duchess wanted a son and had not begun to think of names for a daughter. Whatever was chosen had to be approved by the King. The Duchess wrote, 'I am very anxious to call her Ann Margaret, as I think Ann of York sounds pretty, & Elizabeth and Ann go so well together. I wonder what you think? Lots of people have suggested Margaret, but it has no family links on either side'. The King was against the name Ann and finally, the Duchess wrote to the Queen stating firmly, 'Bertie and I have decided now to call our little daughter Margaret Rose, instead of M. Ann, as Papa does not like the name Ann. I hope you like it. I think that it is very pretty together'.

The Scottish newspapers were quick to point out, approvingly, that there had been a Scottish Queen or Princess with the name 'Margaret' in every generation for the three hundred years between the wife of King Malcolm in the thirteenth century and Margaret Tudor. The baby was named Rose after the Duchess's elder sister, married to William Leveson-Gower, heir presumptive to Earl Granville. On hearing the final choice of names Princess Elizabeth told Lady

51. Princess Margaret on her first birthday, 21 August 1931.

Cynthia Asquith, 'I'm going to call her Bud'. When asked why, Elizabeth replied, 'Well she's not a real rose yet, is she? She's only a bud'.

As 'the Bud' took up most of Alla's time in the nursery, Elizabeth turned to the nursery maid, Margaret MacDonald. This splendid Scotswoman, the daughter of a railway worker from the Black Isle, to the north of Inverness, joined the staff when Elizabeth was a few months old. As under-nurse, she slept in the same bedroom as her charge and when Elizabeth learned to talk, she called her 'Bobo'. Today, Margaret MacDonald is still in the Queen's service as her dresser and is

127

52. Princess Elizabeth leads Princess Margaret's pony, with her favourite groom, Owen, standing by.

probably her closest friend and confidant. Soon after Margaret was born, Bobo's sister, Ruby, was also engaged as nursery-maid and she was to stay with Princess Margaret as maid and then nanny for the next thirty years.

The birth of Margaret seemed to amplify the appeal of her sister in the eyes of the public—initially with dire results. Queen Mary, who had taken it upon herself to instruct her grandchildren, took Elizabeth off to various art galleries, museums and historic sites. On one such trip to the Queen's Hall, Elizabeth was so fidgety that the Queen suggested they go home. Elizabeth replied, 'Oh no, Granny, we can't leave before the end. Think of all the people who'll be waiting to see us outside'. The Queen, horrified, instructed her lady-in-waiting to take Elizabeth out of the back door and home by taxi.

Although 145 Piccadilly was ideal as a London base for the Duke and Duchess of York and their family, they badly needed a place in the country, for the soot-grimed Hamilton Gardens were no substitute for open spaces. The Duke had given up Naseby Hall, having sold all his horses as part of the royal economies at the start of the Depression. The King offered them Royal Lodge, a dilapidated Regency pavilion in Windsor Great Park in September 1931 which they accepted gladly. Once again, the Duchess set about restoring a house and transforming the ruin and garden into an exceptionally pretty and comfortable weekend retreat. Elizabeth had her own house, too, in the grounds of Royal Lodge, a perfect quarter-sized thatched cottage, a sixth birthday present from the people of Wales. It was called 'Y Bwthyn Bach', The Little House. Too small for 'grown-ups', Elizabeth, later with Margaret's help, took great pride in keeping it clean and tidy. It was a wonderful place: 'inside the entrance hall a diminutive grandfather clock tick-tocked softly. The hall table held a tray for visiting-cards and a little bowl of fresh flowers. In the delightful panelled living room everything was in its proper place . . . a painting of the Princess's mother over the fireplace . . . not a speck of dust anywhere . . .'

Interlaced into Elizabeth's trouble-free life were rudimentary lessons from Alla and Bobo, except for reading, which was taught by her mother. It was decided around her sixth birthday that she should have a governess and the Duke, much impressed by Marion Crawford, who taught his sister-in-law's children, asked her to come to Royal Lodge for a month's trial. His choice was right and Elizabeth instantly warmed to this young Scots woman. In September,

53. Princess Elizabeth, aged ten, in front of her miniature Welsh cottage, '*Y Bwthyn Bach*' (The Little House) in the grounds of Royal Lodge in Windsor Great Park.

'Crawfie', as she soon became known, joined the Household full time. She was thoroughly capable and the whole family liked her and found her a bright and sympathetic friend. However, when she left the Household seventeen years later, she earned the Royal Family's scorn by publishing her memoirs giving intimate details of the early life of the Princesses in books and magazine articles.

Crawfie was given a totally free hand in the schoolroom at the top of Royal Lodge and in the Duchess's sitting-room off the drawing-room at 145 Piccadilly. In those revelations, *The Little Princesses*, she wrote,

> No one ever had employers who interfered so little. I had often the feeling that the Duke and Duchess, most happy in their own married life, were not over-concerned with the higher education of their daughters. They wanted most for them a really happy childhood, with lots of pleasant memories stored up against the days that might come and, later, happy marriages.

The King's instructions for his grand-daughter's education were simpler; 'For goodness sake, teach Margaret and Lilibet to write a decent hand, that's all I ask you. None of my children could write properly. They all do it exactly the same way. I like a hand with some character in it.' Queen Mary, on the other hand, took a more positive view of their education and when shown the timetable devised by Crawfie made various suggestions. She thought that there should be more Bible reading and poetry and less arithmetic. Also, in view of Elizabeth's position as third in line of succession, she should have more history, as 'genealogies, historical and dynastic, were very interesting to children'.

As was typical with many nannies with a baby and an older child in the nursery, Alla tried to keep Margaret a baby. Even at the age of two she was still in her pram and, according to Crawfie, she pined to get out and run about. It was Elizabeth, looking for a playmate, who brought her forward, helping her to walk and talk.

The daily routine of the nursery and schoolroom was relaxed. The first 'engagement' was for Elizabeth and Margaret to see their parents in their bedroom, then Elizabeth would be at her lessons by 9.30 until 11. After a glass of orange juice and a biscuit she would play in Hamilton Gardens with her neighbours, usually Lord Allendale's boys, and with her Lascelles and Elphinstone cousins when they were in London. When she was big enough, Margaret joined in games that all children play like 'tag' and 'hopscotch'. Then, before lunch with the Duke and Duchess, if they were 'off duty', half-an-hour was set aside for 'silent reading' and another half-hour when Crawfie read to the girls. They particularly liked A. A. Milne's *Winnie the Pooh* and *When We Were Six*, a present from the Prince of Wales, and when they were older they read some of the classics—Robert Louis Stephenson, Charlotte Brontë and Kipling. Margaret found *Alice in Wonderland* very frightening—'Just imagine as a child reading about some mixture that made you either huge or tiny or running and running and getting nowhere', she said years later. On weekday afternoons, there were either dancing or singing classes. Both Elizabeth and Margaret were very musical. Lady Strathmore remembered carrying downstairs the two-year-old Margaret and to her astonishment heard her humming the *Merry Widow* waltz. Elizabeth was encouraged to read music and not to play by ear, which, with her natural talent and retentive memory, she found easy. Sometimes on Mondays there were instructional visits with Queen Mary to places of historical significance. Occasionally some of their cousins would join Elizabeth and Margaret in the nursery for tea and they would sit round the small table on miniature chairs. A frequent and welcome visitor was their Uncle David, the Prince of Wales. He would stay and play card games with the girls, pelmanism, snap, happy families and racing demon—still the favourite game of the Royal Family. Bath-time was always fun as the Duke and Duchess of York would join them, splashing and playing with their children, then taking them to their room amid shrieks of pleasure, giggles and pillow-fights while Alla would try to quieten her excited charges. When Elizabeth and Margaret were tucked up in bed, 'then arm in arm, the young parents would go downstairs, heated and dishevelled and frequently rather damp . . . The children called to them as they went, until the door finally closed "Good night, Mummie. Good night Papa!"'

Weekends were spent at Royal Lodge. The children, Crawfie, nannies and dogs would pile into a car and be driven down on Friday afternoon. On the Saturday morning the previous week's lessons would be revised but after that, the weekend was spent with their parents. The children, especially Elizabeth, adored horses. From a very early age she kept toy horses on wheels on the landing at 145 Piccadilly outside the nursery and would change the saddles and bridles before bed every night. Her favourite game was to put her sister or Crawfie 'in harness' and drive them about the room. In Windsor Great Park she would ride her pony with her father or with one of the grooms, her favourite being Mr Owen. Elizabeth thought Owen was splendid and in her eyes, everything he did or said was right. On one occasion she asked her father about some future plan to which he replied, 'Don't ask me, ask Owen. Who am I to make suggestions?'

In the early days of Royal Lodge, there was much clearing to do in the garden. Family, staff and guests were roped in to clear and burn the undergrowth. There was always plenty for Elizabeth and Margaret to do at Royal Lodge. Apart from the fun of the little Welsh house, there were the blue budgerigars in their cage to feed and clean, the bird-feeders in the garden to fill or a dog to groom, like Dookie, the first of many corgis, or one of the yellow labradors.

With the help of her sister, Margaret was growing up fast and, from the earliest age displayed that witty, forthright side of her character that is her mark today. At one children's party she was put in the front row of a conjurer's act, so that she could see well. 'No thank you', Margaret replied, 'I shall see *too* well!'

In the mid-1930s, there was a spate of royal occasions, beginning in November 1934 with the wedding in Westminster Abbey of George, Duke of Kent, to Princess Marina of Greece. Elizabeth was chief bridesmaid and 'played her part with dignity and *sangfroid*' and Margaret, clutching her mother's hand tightly, was allowed to attend the ceremony. The Duke and Duchess of York with their daughters drew the largest cheer from the dense crowd that lined the cold London streets. At the balcony appearance, the King lifted Margaret onto the plinth where she waved to the throng below. In that era of Royal Family worship, their appearance on that balcony 'was repayment enough to all who saw it, for whatever hours of waiting it cost them.'

The next ceremony was the twenty-fifth thanksgiving service at St Paul's Cathedral to mark the anniversary of King George V's accession to the throne. The King was greatly moved by the Silver Jubilee celebrations. 'I'm sure I can't understand it,' he told the Archbishop of Canterbury, 'for after all I am only a very ordinary fellow.' The Duke and Duchess of York with their children led the procession and as usual drew the greatest cheer from the crowd. At the Cathedral, they sat, dressed alike in rose pink coats and bonnets, on little stools behind the thrones of their grandparents. At the usual balcony appearance of all the Royal Family, a small hand was seen waving behind the balustrade. A footman brought out a stool and Margaret climbed up and 'as she peered over the balustrade the people shouted with joy and, as the royal group withdrew into the Palace, Princess Margaret lingered awhile and enjoyed the scene by herself.'

The third royal occasion within twelve months was the wedding of Henry, Duke of Gloucester, to Lady Alice Montagu-Douglas-Scott in November 1935. Both Elizabeth and Margaret were chosen as bridesmaids and there was great excitement as they prepared for the wedding and were fitted for their dresses. At the last moment, because of the death of the bride's father, the Duke of Buccleuch, the venue of the wedding was changed from Westminster Abbey to the private chapel at Buckingham Palace. Although the crowd were denied the procession, they cheered as members of the Royal Family made their balcony appearance. 'As always, it was the little Princesses who had the warmest greeting.'

The summer holidays were always spent in Scotland, either at Glamis or Balmoral. Elizabeth and Margaret spent their time very much as their parents had done when they were their age, riding their ponies or bicycles, begging for cakes in the kitchen or dressing up from 'the endless chests full of old-fashioned frocks, and tapestries, and hats of other days, and pieces of silk, and room after room, and passage after passage, in which to play hide-and-seek and sardines'. The Duchess never forgot that her daughters were princesses with royal duties to perform in the future, and one game that would prove useful in later life was charades where she would play the Queen, Prime Minister, foreign potentate or some dignitary and Elizabeth and Margaret had to talk to her with the due deference and respect that her position deserved.

Even during the holidays the children could not escape their lessons. One French mistress at Balmoral so exasperated Elizabeth with her demands for learning columns of irregular verbs that her pupil seized the ink pot and poured blue ink over her own head. Such fits of temper were rare with Elizabeth but, like any girl with a younger sister, she was often goaded into quarrels and fights.

'Margaret always wants everything I want', was a frequent cry. In such fights, Elizabeth would slap her sister while Margaret was prone to biting. When the argument was played out, it would take Elizabeth time to simmer down whereas Margaret recovered instantly with a kiss and a giggle.

According to the Duchess, Margaret took after her father and inherited his temper. It was natural that she, like her father, should feel the frustration of being the younger child, particularly in a royal household where the distinction between children is more marked. Consequently, the Duke tended to spoil her and she responded: 'her father would be almost embarrassed, yet at the same time most touched and pleased; when she wound her arms round his neck, nestled against him and cuddled and caressed him.' This special relationship grew and he delighted in her lively and imaginative mind and her talent as a mimic—very much his own brand of humour.

The Prince of Wales became increasingly jealous of his three younger brothers as they settled into the 'closely-knit fabric of their family lives'. He later wrote of Christmas 1936 at Sandringham, 'I feel lonely and detached, . . . A fourth generation had begun to assert itself . . . Bertie's two children, Elizabeth, who was then nine, and her sister, Margaret Rose, romped around the twenty-foot tree . . .' As a Christmas present that year for all their family, the Duke and Duchess of York had a record made of Elizabeth and Margaret singing a duet of a carol.

Overshadowing that happy family gathering was the reccurrence of the King's bronchial trouble. Shortly after the New Year, Queen Mary called Elizabeth in from the garden and took her upstairs to Grandpapa England's bedroom. She told her that he was very ill indeed and that she should say goodbye to him. Elizabeth and Margaret were sent with Alla and Bobo to Royal Lodge and when the King died on 20 January 1936, the Duchess sent a telegram to Crawfie to return from her holiday to tell the children. 'Don't let all this depress them more than is absolutely necessary, Crawfie', she wrote, 'they are so young.' Elizabeth's reaction was a heartfelt 'Oh Crawfie, ought we to play?' Margaret was thought too young to understand her grandfather's death but she had fixed ideas about Heaven—after her pony Peggy had died, she expected that 'Jesus is riding him, instead of that silly old donkey.' To her, Heaven was like 'a house party where you stayed with God'. She explained to Crawfie, 'Grandpapa is in Heaven now, and I'm sure God finds him very useful!'

Elizabeth, being older, felt the loss more deeply. She went with her mother to Westminster Hall, dressed in a sombre black coat and black velvet tam-o'-shanter, to see the catafalque. Her late grandfather's four sons were standing vigil when she went. Elizabeth was deeply moved and later reported, 'Uncle David was there and he never moved at all, Crawfie. Not even an eyelid. It was wonderful. And everyone was so quiet. As if the King was asleep.'

The main effects on Elizabeth and Margaret of the accession of the Prince of Wales to the throne were that he no longer dropped in on their nursery and that they saw him less often. Now that he was King Edward VIII, his life-style was very different to that of his father which in turn distanced him from his brothers, in particular the Duke of York. The Princesses still enjoyed their weekends at Royal Lodge and the summer in Scotland at Glamis and Birkhall, but they missed the enjoyable visits they used to make to Balmoral and Windsor Castle and Sandringham.

As the Court was in morning for six months for the King, dancing classes for Elizabeth and Margaret were postponed, but the time was usefully filled by swimming lessons from a Miss Amy Daly at the Bath Club. The pupils were keen to be like any other and chose the regulation Bath Club dark blue costume with white initials and cap. Elizabeth 'looked so pretty in hers. She was a long slender child with beautiful legs. Margaret, everyone owned, looked like a plump navy-blue fish.' When they could swim, the girls enjoyed their afternoons at the Bath Club. The Duke and Duchess came to see them and the Duke remarked, 'I don't know how they do it. We were always so terribly shy and self-conscious as children. These two don't seem to care.'

The world of the childrens' nursery was far removed from the constitutional crisis that raged in their parents' world but Elizabeth, and to a lesser degree Margaret, were aware that something unusual was happening. They saw the headlines in the newspapers speculating on the future of the King and Mrs Simpson and on the possibility of his abdication. They watched a steady stream of solemn dignitaries and politicians as they walked across the hall of 145 Piccadilly to their father's study. To make matters worse for their father, the Duchess was in bed with a heavy cold. Crowds began to gather outside their house and as the abdication grew inevitably closer shouts of 'Long live King Albert', the name it was assumed he would adopt, were heard in the nursery on the top floor.

King Edward VIII signed the instruments of abdication at his house, Fort Belvedere, in Windsor Great Park, and the next day, 11 December 1936, the instruments were ratified by Parliament. The Duke and Duchess of York now became King George VI and Queen Elizabeth, and the young Elizabeth, four months away from her eleventh birthday, was heir presumptive. Crawfie broke the news to the children whose main concern was that they would have to leave their cosy existence at 145 Piccadilly and move to Buckingham Palace. 'You mean for ever?' was Elizabeth's reply. To Margaret, the change of her parents' rôle had a more practical aspect. 'I have only just learned how to spell York—Y-O-R-K— and now I am not to use it any more. I am to sign myself Margaret all alone.'

Two days later, their father left in his uniform as Admiral of the Fleet for the Accession Council traditionally held in St James's Palace. Crawfie explained that on his return Elizabeth and Margaret should curtsey to him and their mother. So, when the King entered the hall, 'both little girls swept him a beautiful curtsey. I think perhaps that nothing that had occurred had brought the change in his condition to him as clearly as this did. He stood for a moment touched and taken aback.' Then he stopped and kissed them both warmly.

54. A sleepy Princess Margaret, overawed by the Coronation of her father as King George VI, rests her head on the edge of the Royal Box at Westminster Abbey. With her are Queen Mary, her sister Princess Elizabeth and aunt Princess Mary.

Elizabeth's sentiments for 145 Piccadilly were well-founded for Buckingham Palace was still uncomfortable. Electricity had only recently been installed and for the most part it was vast and draughty.

There were so many mice that a full-time 'vermin-man' was employed to keep the mouse population within a reasonable level. Elizabeth, with her love of animals, was horrified at his job. The King and Queen moved into the Palace in February 1937 and their daughters and nursery staff followed soon after. The many toy horses went, too, and were stabled in the corridor outside Elizabeth's room and remained there right up to the time she married ten years later.

It was inevitable that now Elizabeth was heir presumptive she should receive greater exposure to the public and be treated differently to her sister. For instance, in the order of service for mattins, the prayer for the Royal Family named 'Princess Elizabeth' but not Margaret. When the new King and Queen reviewed the Fleet at Spithead, it was only Elizabeth who was seen beside her parents; likewise when they went to open the new Maritime Museum at Greenwich, Margaret was left at home. It was not now easy for their parents to treat the sisters the same, even though it was still very much their policy. The girls were still dressed identically and their routine in the nursery differed only through age rather than rank—Margaret supposedly went to bed half-an-hour earlier than her sister. Their characters, too, were very different. Elizabeth was a neat, methodical child, often hopping 'out of bed several times a night to get her shoes quite straight and her clothes arranged just so.' It was Margaret, actor and mimic, who cured many of those fads with her impersonations.

Part of the problem of trying to bring up two Princesses, one of whom was heir presumptive, as ordinary children, was that they simply were not ordinary. Their life behind the railings of Buckingham Palace was restrictive and their world revolved round their parents and their parents' friends, the schoolroom and the nursery, and Crawfie, Alla and Bobo. In the holidays there were plenty of cousins to play with—the Elphinstones, the Leveson-Gowers, the Lascelles and the Bowes-Lyons, all of whom, in varying degrees, formed the nucleus of their friends in later life. Margaret, with her inventive mind and loneliness, conjured up a 'Cousin Halifax'. Cousin Halifax was the answer to everything; he made her late, he lost the dog's lead, he had a cold so they could not go on some unwelcome trip.

Sensing the effect of the lack of friends in London and Windsor, their parents decided that it could be partially overcome by forming a Girl Guides' pack, the 1st Buckingham Palace Company. The troop was made up of the children of friends of their parents and initially was not a success. The nannies who brought their charges treated it as just another form of dancing-class but when the children of the Palace staff and houshold joined, it soon livened up. Margaret was too young to join and a pack of Brownies was formed for her. Both girls loved their afternoons of cooking on open fires, practising first aid and playing games with their fellow Guides. The only disappointment was that the meetings were held too infrequently.

The Coronation of King Edward VIII had originally been set for 12 May 1937 and that date was kept for his brother. The preparations for the great day occupied the Princesses fully. Lessons were allied to the history and symbolism of the Coronation and even French lessons took on a new twist. When Elizabeth welcomed the French President, Monsieur Lebrun, in a carefully prepared speech, he was much impressed when she continued to talk to him in good conversational French.

On the morning of the Coronation, Elizabeth took an exercise book and wrote an essay in red crayon entitled, 'The Coronation, 12 May, 1937. To Mummy and Papa. In Memory of their Coronation, From Lillibet By Herself.' The essay, kept in the Royal Library at Windsor tied up with a piece of pink ribbon, begins,

At five o'clock in the morning I was woken up by the band of the Royal Marines just outside my window. I leapt out of bed and so did Bobo. We put on our dressing gowns and shoes and Bobo made me put on an eiderdown as it was so cold and we crouched in the window looking on to a cold misty morning. There were already some people in the stands and all the time people were coming to them in a stream with occasional pauses in between. Every now and then we were hopping out of bed looking at the bands and the soldiers. At six o'clock Bobo got up and instead of getting up at my usual time I jumped out of bed at half-past seven. When I was going to the bathroom I passed the lift, as usual, and who should walk out but Miss Daly! [her swimming instructress from the Bath Club] I was very pleased to see her. When I dressed I went into the nursery.

In keeping with their parents' intention that the two sisters should be treated exactly alike, Elizabeth and Margaret's Coronation robes and coronets were, as with all their other clothes, identical. Their dresses were of lace with tiny silver bows and their cloaks were edged with ermine. When Elizabeth went to see Crawfie she lifted her skirts to show off her silver slippers and the governess noted that she was wearing 'the short white socks of childhood' underneath.

Elizabeth feared that her sister would let the side down. 'I hope she won't disgrace us by falling asleep in the middle', she said gravely. 'After all she is very young for a Coronation.' Fortunately she was wrong and she reported later that 'I only had to nudge her once or twice while she played with her prayer books too loudly.' The two Princesses were a tremendous success. They travelled to Westminster Abbey in the Glass Coach with Queen Mary and Queen Maud (Queen of Norway, her sister-in-law), Margaret sitting on a specially built-up seat so that she could see out and wave to the cheering crowds.

55. Princess Elizabeth with her cousin, Lady Jane Cambridge, at Buckingham Palace.

56. Queen Elizabeth with her daughters—Princess Elizabeth in Girl Guide's uniform and Princess Margaret as a Brownie.

After the Coronation, the lives of the 'Little Princesses' continued much as before although for Elizabeth and occasionally Margaret as well, there would always be some official function to attend—the State Opening of Parliament, a garden party, the review of a regiment or an official visit to some part of the country. They were still too young to accompany their parents on their tour of Canada and the United States of America in May 1939. President Roosevelt explained to their parents: 'If you bring either or both of the children they will also be very welcome, and I shall try to have one or two Roosevelts of approximately the same age to play with them!' The King and Queen left for seven weeks on the *Empress of Australia* on May 5 and Elizabeth and Margaret went with Queen Mary to see them off. On the quay, Margaret said, 'I have my handkerchief!' to which Elizabeth replied, 'To wave, not to cry.'

Elizabeth had just had her thirteenth birthday before her parents left for America. Outwardly, she was a confident child, fulfilling splendidly her role as heir presumptive to the throne. Behind that display of confidence, however, she

57. Members of the Royal Family watch the departure of King George VI and Queen Elizabeth on their tour of North America, 1939. From left to right, the Duke and Duchess of Kent, The Princess Royal, the Duchess of Gloucester, Queen Mary and the Princesses Margaret and Elizabeth.

was a placid girl, somewhat shy like her father. Because of her upbringing and the parity with her sister, like their clothes of 'uniform tweed coats, simple collars, berets, white socks and plain sandals', she had not matured physically as fast as other girls of her age 'when so many are gawky, yet she was an enchanting child with the loveliest hair and skin and the loveliest figure.'

While the King and Queen were in America, a treat was organised for Elizabeth and Margaret, a journey by London's Underground to visit the Young Womens' Christian Association in the Tottenham Court Road. What would appear today as a chore was then, to girls with a closeted upbringing, an exciting adventure. It was a novel experience, too, for Crawfie, born and bred in Scotland, and for Lady Helen Graham, the Queen's lady-in-waiting. They bought their own tickets at St James's station, then, having had advice from the Palace staff days before on how best to cope with a moving staircase, they confidently took the escalator down to the platform. It was a thrilling experience for them all, 'the train rushing out of the tunnel and the sliding doors opening as if by magic'. Once inside the train, a man was at first amazed to find himself the

58. Princess Elizabeth, front left, before a children's swimming competition at the Bath Club, London, 1939.

centre of attention only to realise that it was really the two little girls beside him, their tickets clasped tightly in their hands, who were the focus of curiosity. At Tottenham Court Road station, the press were there to meet them and they walked to the YWCA in a barrage of flash bulbs. Because of that, the experiment was never repeated.

In keeping with Elizabeth's role as heir presumptive, the Queen decided that she needed a wider education than Crawfie could give her and so the eminent historian, Henry Marten, vice-provost of Eton, was chosen for the task. He was a charming man and a popular history master, despite a strange habit of chewing his handkerchief in between munching sugar lumps while teaching. At first Elizabeth was nervous of him and of his study overflowing with books but they soon developed a very close working relationship that was to continue for many years. She flourished under his tutelage and later, after the outbreak of the Second World War when she was in Scotland, the lessons continued by post.

The summer holidays of 1939 began soon after their parents returned from America and Elizabeth and Margaret sailed in the Royal Yacht, the *Victoria and Albert*, along the south coast of England and entered the River Dart estuary on 22 July. The King, accompanied by his cousin, Lord Louis Mountbatten, was keen to return to their 'old school', the Royal Naval College, Dartmouth. During the two-day visit to the college, 'Uncle Dicky' Mountbatten's nephew, Prince Philip of Greece, was detailed to entertain the Princesses at the Captain's House. On doctors' advice, they were kept apart from the rest of the party as there was a twin epidemic of mumps and chicken-pox raging in the college. Philip was enthusiastic and eager to please and Elizabeth seemed enraptured by him. Again it was Crawfie who recorded that first meeting:

> She never took her eyes off him the whole time. At the tennis courts I thought he showed off a good deal, but the little girls were much impressed. Lilibet said, "How good he is, Crawfie! How high he can jump!" He was quite polite to her but did not pay her any special attention. He spent a lot of time teasing plump little Margaret.

That night, Philip dined aboard the Royal Yacht but Elizabeth, still only thirteen, kept nursery hours and was in bed well before dinner. They were to meet the next day at tea where 'Philip had several platefuls of shrimps, and a banana split, among other trifles. To the little girls a boy of any kind was always a strange creature out of another world. Lilibet sat, pink-faced, enjoying it all very much. To Margaret, anyone who could eat so many shrimps was a hero.'

When the *Victoria and Albert* prepared to leave, every boat at the college had been mustered to escort the Royal Yacht down the river. When they reached the sea, the King signalled for the flotilla to return. One solitary rowing-boat followed well out into the open sea. The King turned to Vice-Admiral Sir Dudley North, commander of the Royal Yacht, and said, 'The damned young fool! He must go back. We must heave to otherwise and send him back.' Philip finally obeyed and later admitted that he only wanted to show his respect for the King.

Elizabeth 'watched him fondly through an enormous pair of binoculars' until she could no longer make out the speck on the horizon.

Elizabeth was thirteen-and-a-half years old and Margaret four years younger when war was declared on 3 September 1939. Elizabeth's reaction to the news was, 'More history for children to learn in a hundred years time', then added 'I don't think people should talk about battles and things in front of Margaret, we don't want to upset her.' They were staying at Birkhall, their house on the Balmoral estate, and the King and Queen decided to leave them there on an extended holiday. Crawfie was brought back from her holiday and the school routine continued as if nothing had happened. She kept the same timetable with the same breaks and walks over the estate. At six o'clock precisely they would talk to their parents on the telephone.

A French mistress, a Mrs Montaudon-Smith familiarly known as 'Monty', was brought in to help Crawfie with the lessons while the history papers still came regularly by post from Henry Marten. Elizabeth and Margaret's time at Birkhall was not all school work. They helped with the activities organised for the evacuees from Glasgow, they joined the local Girl Guides Company—also swelled with Glaswegian girls—and they rehearsed for a nativity play that was never actually performed because of a case of mumps in the village. There were also trips to Aberdeen to the dentist and Christmas shopping at Woolworths.

The children missed their parents dreadfully and the Queen was worried about the particularly harsh winter in that part of Scotland. At Birkhall, the main rooms were warm enough with their open log fires but elsewhere it was freezing. To Margaret's delight, her face-flannel once froze solid. At last the Queen announced that her daughters could come south for the traditional Christmas at Sandringham. Although Sandringham, close to the north Norfolk coast, was an easy prey to Nazi attack, the King and Queen thought it worth the risk. It was a memorable and happy time and the children delighted their parents by singing a duet in French that Monty had taught them. It was from here, too, that the King made the first of his live wartime Christmas Day broadcasts, a great ordeal in view of his stammer, which he successfully overcame.

There was no doubt that Elizabeth and Margaret were in danger throughout the whole of the war, if not from Nazi paratrooper attack, from bombers en route for Bristol or the Midlands. An easy solution would have been to evacuate them to Canada like thousands of other children. This, however, was not acceptable to the King and Queen and their daughters stayed in the country. The Queen announced that, 'The children won't leave without me; I won't leave without the King; and the King will never leave.' Elizabeth and Margaret moved first to Royal Lodge, described as 'a house somewhere in the country', but after the invasion of Holland by German forces on 12 May 1940, the Queen ordered that they should move to Windsor Castle. They occupied their usual rooms in the Lancaster Tower, and, despite the new surroundings, soon reverted to the orderly, regulated tempo of their earlier life. In those early days at Windsor, Elizabeth and Margaret kept adult company, first with the Master of their

Household, the sixty-year-old Brigadier-General Sir Hill Child, and Lord Wigram, Governor of the Tower, then with the officers from the Grenadier Guards stationed at Windsor. Elizabeth, aged fourteen, played hostess to them all in a manner far beyond her years, talking intelligently and coping well in the way she had learnt from her mother. Three officers would lunch with them every day, sometimes taking tea as well. Margaret's end of the table was never quiet and one officer remembers that 'the conversation never lapsed for a moment. She was amazingly self-assured, without being embarrassingly so.' Later they joined the local Girl Guides and mixed happily with the Cockney refugees who were rather more in their own age group.

The value of the Royal Family to the Empire during the war was inestimable. Elizabeth's first contribution came on 13 October 1940 when she made a live broadcast on Children's Hour. She wrote the script herself and was rehearsed by the Queen until she had the tempo and her breathing absolutely right. 'I can truthfully say to you all,' she read, 'that we children at home are full of cheerfulness and courage. We are trying to do all we can to help our gallant sailors, soldiers and airmen, and we are trying, too, to bear our share of the

59. Princess Elizabeth at the microphone when she broadcast on Children's Hour, October 1940. Her sister, Princess Margaret, literally had the last word.

143

60. The family gathering—Elizabeth knitting watched by her mother, Queen Elizabeth and sister, Princess Margaret with their father, King George VI, 1942.

danger and sadness of war. We know, every one of us, that in the end all will be well.' It was a confident delivery without hesitation or apparent nervousness. Elizabeth concluded the speech by saying, 'My sister is by my side, and we are both going to say goodnight to you. Come on, Margaret.' Margaret piped up and ended the broadcast with 'Goodnight children, and good luck to you all.' It was a great morale-booster throughout the Empire and the free world.

Like everyone in the country, Elizabeth and Margaret acclimatized themselves to wartime austerity. In common with every other house, Windsor Castle was cold, the windows blacked out, with dim electric light bulbs and single-bare electric fires. Windsor Castle was made even more bleak by the removal of the rugs and carpets from the corridors, and the pictures were taken down and the furniture stored. When they went for a walk in Windsor Great Park, Elizabeth and Margaret were shadowed by a tank and at the moment an enemy fighter was sighted, the tank would take them back to the safety of the Castle, protected by 'the Bofors boys'—a light anti-aircraft battery.

At the all-too-common mournful wail of the air-raid sirens, Elizabeth and

Margaret would descend into the cellars that served as a shelter along with the rest of the household—a proper shelter was built later with bedrooms and a bathroom for members of the Royal Family. When the very first warning sounded, Crawfie, her responsibility for the Princesses over at six o'clock, went to the shelter. When she discovered that the girls were not there she

> ran to the nurseries where I could hear a great deal of commotion going on. I shouted 'Alah' [sic] . . . Alah was always very careful. Her cap had to be put on, and her white uniform. Lilibet called, 'We're dressing, Crawfie, we must dress.' I said 'Nonsense! You are not to dress. Put a coat over your night clothes, at once.' They finally came to the shelter. By this time Sir Hill Child was a nervous wreck. He stood rather in awe of Alah, but he said, 'You must understand that the Princesses must come down at once. They must come down whatever they are wearing.' . . . The little girls were very good. They took it all most calmly. Margaret fell asleep on my knee. Lilibet lay down and read a book. . . . At two o'clock Sir Hill Child bowed ceremoniously to Lilibet. 'You may now go to bed, Ma'am,' he said.

Throughout most of the war, the King and Queen remained in London at Buckingham Palace and drove down to Windsor for the weekends. Without her parents, Elizabeth developed rapidly in her new rôle during the week as 'mistress' of the Castle. Her parents noticed the change, and they discussed in detail with her the developments of the war and affairs of state, the King always mindful of the role his daughter was to play in later life.

One of the great events during the wartime years at Windsor was the pantomime. It started as a nativity play, *The Little Child*, with Margaret cast in the title role, and Elizabeth as a king, with two evacuees and the boys from the local school making up the rest of the cast. After seeing the performance and hearing Margaret singing a solo, 'Gentle Jesus meek and mild', the King wrote in his diary that night, 'I wept through most of it. It is such a wonderful story'. Full-scale pantomimes followed, *Cinderella* in 1941, *The Sleeping Beauty* the year after, *Aladdin* the Christmas after that and, finally, *Old Mother Red Riding Boots* in 1944. They were a tremendous success and Elizabeth, Margaret and the rest of the cast enjoyed them enormously. They charged an entry fee and the sum total of all performances netted £850 for the Queen's Wool Fund.

At the last performance of *Old Mother Red Riding Boots* Crawfie noticed that Elizabeth's performance was better than ever: 'I have never known her more animated. There was a sparkle about her none of us had ever seen before. Many people remarked on it.' The reason for that sparkle was the fair-haired Philip, home on leave from the Royal Navy, sitting in the front row. They were to see each other occasionally and correspond in a 'cousinly fashion' when he was away.

When Elizabeth was eighteen, her father could no longer ignore her pleas to 'join up' in the services. She saw it as a chance to escape the confines of her restricted life and an opportunity to do some 'real war-work'. She was granted an honorary commission in the Auxiliary Territorial Service at Aldershot as

61. Princess Margaret, far left, in the Windsor Pantomime, 'Old Mother Red Riding Boots', December 1944.

No. 230873, Second Subaltern Elizabeth Alexandra Mary Windsor. Age: 18. Eyes: blue. Hair: brown. Height: 5 ft 3 ins. The idea was that she would be treated like any other ATS officer and sleep at Aldershot but in practice she slept at Windsor Castle and was driven every day to attend her course on heavy vehicle maintenance, driving, map-reading and how to strip and service an engine. She greatly enjoyed her work and went at it in a typically determined fashion.

No sooner had Elizabeth gained her new-found freedom with the ATS than the war drew to a close. VE Day (Victory-Europe) was declared on 8 May 1945. The whole country went wild and the national thanksgiving was led by King George VI. Buckingham Palace was almost under siege by a gigantic and ecstatic crowd, all clamouring to see the King and Queen and their daughters. They made eight balcony appearances during the afternoon and early evening, some with the Prime Minister, Winston Churchill. That evening, with the Mall still packed with happy revellers under the bright lights that had been extinguished for five-and-a-half years, the King detailed two officers to take Elizabeth and Margaret out of a side door of the Palace to mingle with the crowd. The

62. Second Subaltern Elizabeth Windsor, No 230873, carries out essential maintenance on an Army truck, Aldershot 1945.

Princesses were swept along in that human tide, declaring later that they 'never had such a beautiful evening'.

The First World War had robbed the Queen Elizabeth of the youthful enjoyment of her adolescent years. With that experience behind her, she knew how to help her own children though the wartime years of 1939–45, although her first duty was of course to her husband. Despite all the pressures, she was able to create a secure, loving and happy home. Guided by her, her daughters emulated her charm, wisdom and deep faith and, in general, the lighter sides of their characters also stem from her. King George VI, remembering his own childhood, sought to protect the womenfolk from his own personal anxieties and those of his office. Occasionally, these pent-up emotions and worries would come out in a frightening display of temper, rarely with his family, although the effect of these explosions could be felt by them. He believed, and succeeded, in making his family life 'fun'. Above all, he instilled into his daughters his unswerving devotion to duty. The success of Princess Elizabeth as Queen can be squarely attributed not only to that happy childhood and moral code of her loving parents, but also to her husband, that Dartmouth cadet, whom she had loved from their first meeting, Prince Philip.

5

Prince Philip

At the wedding reception in 1934 of George, Duke of Kent, and Princess Marina of Greece, King George V went up to a tall, fair-haired youth of thirteen and remarked, 'You're Andrew's boy'. The King's identification was correct as he was addressing Prince Philip, son of Prince Andrew of Greece and Princess Alice of Battenburg. 'Andrew's boy' was related to practically every Royal guest in the room, being directly descended from the 'grandfather of Europe', King Christian IX, on his father's side and the 'grandmother of Europe', Queen Victoria, through his mother; a noble ancestry that can even be traced back to Charlemagne.

Yet Philip was born in comparatively modest surroundings on the island of Corfu. His parents had inherited an attractive neo-classical villa with the unlikely name of 'Mon Repos'. The house, built for the British High Commissioner to the Ionian Islands in the 1820s, was far from grand. It was hardly large enough for their existing family of four daughters, Margarita, Theodora, Cecilie and Sophie—nicknamed Tiny—and their staff, just a Scottish couple called Blower. There was a sunny entrance hall with a wide staircase to the first floor and four bedrooms and two box-rooms in the attic above. On the ground floor was Prince Andrew's study next to the dining-room then the drawing-room with its French windows opening onto the pretty garden. By contemporary standards, 'Mon Repos' was primitive. There was only cold water, no electricity and no form of heating against the damp winters. Water had to be heated on a coal-burning range in the kitchen and carried upstairs every time anyone wanted a bath. While the house lacked comfort, the setting was perfection. It stood in a wild but beautiful garden on a promontory overlooking the straights between mainland Greece and the island. Paths led through orange and lemon groves, past sweet-smelling eucalyptus, gnarled olive trees and tall cypresses down to the rocks and sea below. It was an idyllic place, especially in summer, but the beauty and tranquillity belied the tension of the troubled times in Greece in mid-1921. The monarchy, with its Danish origins and strong German connections, was decidedly unpopular and the country was at war, disastrously, with Turkey. Prince Andrew, a lieutenant-general commanding

63. 'Mon Repos', Corfu, the birthplace of Prince Philip.

the Third Army Corps, was dispatched to the front, leaving his wife and family at home.

At dawn on Friday 10 June 1921, the local doctor from Corfu town was summoned to 'Mon Repos' for the delivery of Princess Alice's baby. For some reason, he decided that her bedroom was unsuitable and she was carried downstairs and placed on the dining-room table. There, at ten o'clock in the morning on a white embroidered table cloth, she gave birth to a healthy and well-formed boy with 'a whispery down of ash blond hair on his head'. The

149

doctor was assisted by the two eldest daughters, aged sixteen and fifteen, and their English nanny, Miss Roose.

Miss Roose, affectionately known as 'Roosie' to all the family, had come to Princess Alice from looking after her brother-in-law Nicholas's three girls, Olga, Elizabeth and Marina, the future Duchess of Kent. She was a splendid, matronly woman, with a strong belief in all things British. Weeks before the birth she demanded that Lord Louis Mountbatten, Princess Alice's younger brother, should send supplies of tinned baby food, soap and knitted baby clothes from London. She distrusted the Greek food prepared by a Corfiot cook, preferring to serve her latest charge with 'nourishing rice and tapioca puddings and good wholesome Scots porridge'. Philip flourished on this imported diet, but, because of the family's impecunious state, there were no other frills to his life. According to Agnes Blower, the housekeeper, 'They did not live like Royals. . . . They were as poor as church mice.' Years later, she remembered that Philip had no toys save for some 'red, white and blue bricks, roughly hewn from some old pieces of timber by a young gardener . . . His favourite toy was his nanny's pin cushion. For hours he sat quietly in his cot, pulling the pins and needles out and pushing them in again. I was always worried that he would hurt himself'.

When Philip was twelve weeks old, his maternal grandfather, Prince Louis of Battenburg, Admiral and former First Lord of the Admiralty, died. (During the First World War the Battenburgs had anglicised their name to Mountbatten and Prince Louis was created the first Marquess of Milford Haven.) Princess Alice, Roosie and all the children travelled to England for the funeral and the Princess was proud to show off her son, the sixth in line to the Greek throne, to her family. By the time they returned to Corfu, Prince Andrew was back from the war and saw his baby for the first time.

Princess Alice returned to England with her family a year later for the wedding of her younger brother, Lord Louis Mountbatten, to Edwina Ashley. The four sisters were bridesmaids but Philip, being at a 'climbing up' stage, remained behind at Kensington Palace. The Princess wanted to stay longer in London, but news that the war with Turkey was going badly for Greece made her return to Corfu.

The Army, in particular the Third Corps, had suffered catastrophic losses. Prince Andrew, its commander, against his better judgement, was forced by the Government into a disastrous engagement. After the crashing defeat of the Greek Army in August 1922 and the subsequent sacking of Smyrna, a revolutionary council deposed King Constantine in favour of his son George. Prince Andrew was allowed to return to his family in Corfu with the assurance from the revolutionary council that they would be left in peace. His stay at 'Mon Repos' was brief, however, for he was required to give evidence at the trial of various 'royal traitors'. When he arrived in Athens, he was immediately arrested and charged, along with the Commander-in-Chief and other generals, three ex-Premiers and various members of the cabinet, with the calamitous results of the war. Six of the accused had already been executed before a firing squad by the

64. Prince Philip, aged one, at the wedding of his uncle, Lord Louis Mountbatten, July 1922.

time his trial was set for 2 December and Prince Andrew philosophically awaited death. He did not, however, allow for the fortitude of his wife. Leaving Philip and his sisters at 'Mon Repos', she rushed to Athens, and appealed to the revolutionary council for her husband's life. When that produced no results she canvassed the Pope, King Alphonso of Spain, and her brother, Lord Louis Mountbatten, who talked with King George V. A former naval attaché in Athens Embassy, Commander Gerald Talbot, travelled secretly to Athens and extracted a promise from the Greek Minister of War that, although Prince Andrew would be found guilty on totally spurious charges and in all probability sentenced to death, he would in fact be handed over to him. At the trial, Prince Andrew was indeed found guilty and sentenced to imprisonment, deprived of his rank and title and banished from Greece for life, but the Greek council kept their word and Talbot took Prince Andrew to the cruiser *Calypso* where Princess Alice was waiting. On the way to Brindisi, the *Calypso* anchored off Corfu. Philip in

Roosie's arms, his sisters and a few of their possessions were taken on board. To make Philip comfortable, the sailors lined an orange box for the eighteen-month-old child—his very first and somewhat humiliating taste of the Royal Navy.

After a brief audience with the Pope in the Vatican, the deposed family of Prince and Princess Andrew arrived in London and moved into the apartments at Kensington Palace lent by her mother, the Dowager Marchioness of Milford Haven. Although the accomodation was cramped, Philip and his sisters enjoyed themselves. Christmas brought the whole family together and Philip met his cousins and the two Mountbatten uncles who would have such a marked influence on him in later life. In the New Year of 1923 his parents left for America to stay with his uncle, Prince Christopher, and his heiress wife, Nancy. Their trip merely postponed Prince Andrew's more pressing problems—the question of his nationality and the means to house and support his family. The first was solved when his cousin, King Christian X of Denmark, granted his whole family Danish passports. But his cash crisis remained.

Princess Alice's family helped but their modest gifts barely covered the girls' school fees. More substantial assistance finally came from his brother, Prince George, whose wife, Princess Marie Bonaparte, was immensely rich through a maternal grandfather who owned the Casino at Monte Carlo. He offered them a suite of rooms in their house in rue Adolphe Ivan close to the Bois de Boulogne in Paris. Despite various inheritances they could not afford the staff that went with the house and moved to a small, but attractive lodge in the apple orchard of the house where Prince George actually lived in the rue de Mont Valerien in St Cloud. For some years to come, this was home to Philip.

After such an inauspicious start to his life, Philip now grew up in a safe and generally loving atmosphere. Being the youngest in a family of girls, he was inevitably spoiled by the ever-faithful Roosie and his mother, although his sisters were sometimes 'very anxious to prevent it and were all particularly disagreeable and strict to him'. Apart from these occasional outbursts from his sisters, he enjoyed the attentions of a host of family friends who doted on him and he repaid their affection in kind. Although he would display his independence, being 'very pugnacious' so that 'the other children were scared to death of him', he was like many another small boy, daring and mischievous but kind and well-mannered as well.

From a very early age, Philip spent the holidays, especially the summer holidays, with various relations throughout Europe accompanied by his sisters, Roosie and his mother. There were frequent visits to Panka on the Baltic, the summer residence of the late King Constantine's widow, the former Princess Sophie of Prussia. It was a wonderful place, right on the sea, with a criss-cross of paths leading through the gardens and woods or down to the home farm. There were expeditions to the beach and, with his cousin Alexandra, he would splash about the water's edge and swim, sometimes fully clothed. They would explore the tiny port with its fishing boats and stalwart fisherman. There is no doubt that Philip's love for the sea stems from his experience of that coastline.

Prince Philip

This love of water, however, did not extend to bathtime. Philip, being the youngest, was bathed first and invariably, when dressed only in his vest, he would escape as Nanny Roose tested the temperature of the bath water. Then the fun would start. Philip would run all over the house, chased by the septuagenarian Roosie—to the delight of everyone, children and 'grown-ups' alike, except of course for Roosie.

The holidays are well chronicled by Philip's cousin, Alexandra, later to become Queen Alexandra of Yugoslavia. One of her recollections was of their stay at Panka when they sneaked into the piggeries at the home farm. They decided to open the doors to see what would happen but

> the pigs went on grunting and browsing and paying no heed. It was almost as boring as if we were with the grown-ups on the lawn having tea, listening to the meaningless conversation tinkling over our heads. To stir events up Philip took a stick to the pigs—and then pandemonium broke loose with a fury of movement and sound. Squealing, screaming, freed from their sties, the pigs stampeded and scampered past the fodder-barn towards the tea-lawn. We could no more control their closed ranks than control the wind. Between the elegant little chairs and tables the pigs rushed, upsetting trays and tea-things. I remember aunts and uncles screaming, shouting and running while dismayed servants rushed hither and thither, baffled by the swarming tide. It was wonderful while it lasted. Carried on by the wild excitement we two children, alas, betrayed ourselves.

Retribution was eventually shared and, by all accounts, was none too serious.

Philip also visited his English relations and stayed with his Uncle George, the second Marquess of Milford Haven at his home on the River Thames, Lynden Manor, near Maidenhead. They were particularly happy days as he grew close to his uncle and enjoyed the company of his cousin, David and his elder sister, Tatiana. Another favourite visit was to Rumanian relatives, King Carol and Queen Helen and their son, Michael, an exact contemporary of Philip's. Splendid times were spent at their palace of Cotrocene near Bucharest or at their summer houses on the Black Sea or in the cool hills at Sinaia. When Michael became King of Rumania on the death of his grandfather it 'made no difference to our play'. Joined by Alexandra, the three cousins would ride their horses or bicycles, swim in or row on the lakes. It was not long before Philip began to emerge as the leader, organising the pony races on the beach or rounding up others into teams of sand-castle builders.

One special place where Philip often stayed in the summer holidays was in the south of France at Berck-Plage, near Marseilles. The fabulous house and estate belonged to a Madame Foufounis, the widow of a Greek loyalist who had befriended the exiled Prince Andrew and his family. Madame Foufounis had two children, a son, Jean, a contemporary of Philip's and his sister, Hélène, well-known in later life as the singer, Hélène Cordet. Despite their impecunious state compared to the immense wealth of the Foufounis, Hélène believed 'the little blue-eyed boy with the most fascinating blond-white hair seemed to have everything I lacked. In my mind he became a great danger, and I became ridiculously jealous.' Philip displayed a 'passion for going round the farm, feeding the pigs and cleaning the pigsties'. It was at Berck-Plage that the generous side of his character came out. A guest to the house brought a present for each of the children except Ria, the youngest who was an invalid and probably unknown to the guest. On seeing that she was without a present, Philip not only immediately gave her his new toy but rushed inside to fetch all his old ones as well.

Schooling proper for Philip started when he was nearly six. His mother had already taught him to read but she had strangely neglected writing and she now chose the progressive American Country Day and Boarding School in St Cloud for her son, which was near enough for Philip to walk there with a sister or servant. His mother hoped that Philip would 'have his future in an English-speaking country', for the school catered mostly for the sons of American ex-patriots and diplomats. The heavy fees were conveniently paid by the heiress Nancy, the American wife of Prince Christopher, who had never met her nephew.

The school house, better known as the 'Elms' from the large trees in the ample gardens, had once belonged to the writer Jules Verne. It was run by Donald and Charlotte MacJannet who, like most of the staff and pupils, were American. From April 1929, Philip was taught by a Catherine Pegg. On the first morning she asked her class their names:

> The seventh boy, blond, blue-eyed, looking very much like an English prep-school boy in his grey flannels and striped tie, introduced himself with an angelic smile as simply 'Philip'.
> 'Philip what?' I asked.
> 'Just Philip,' came the reply gently.
> 'But you must have some other name', I answered.
> 'Philip of Greece', he murmured in an embarrassed whisper, and let the matter drop.

It was not long before Philip was speaking English with an American accent and playing baseball and American football. Catherine Pegg recorded that he was competitive, rushing 'across the sports ground, taking a tumble here and there, only looking rather disconsolate if he happened to tear his plus-fours, for his wardrobe was not extensive and he told me that his mother would remonstrate if he came home with torn clothes'. His sweaters were already darned and he had no raincoat until he bought one for himself out of the pocket money, birthday and Christmas money from his innumerable relations which he had carefully saved. A bicycle came later out of his savings.

Even at that age, Philip had a great sense of duty. Miss Pegg remembered him sitting on her right for meals,

> not as an honoured guest but because he was a particularly agile and careful carrier of hot dishes. He never would wait for the maid to carry in the different courses,

for, as he explained to me, his mother had taught him that a gentleman does not allow women to wait on him . . . Often he would remain after school was over to chat with me as I corrected exercises. He instituted himself as class monitor and without being asked, would straighten the desks, collect waste paper, water the plants and think out different ways of making our school more attractive . . .

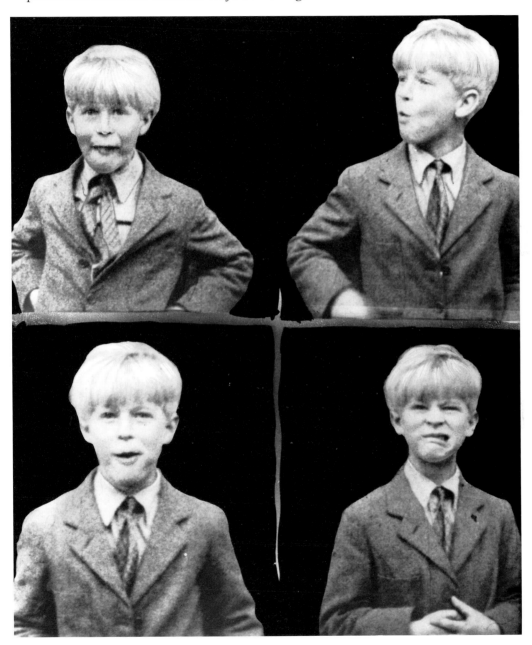

65. A biscuit-eating competition was organised at the American Country Day School in St Cloud, Paris, 1928, where Philip was a pupil.

66. Prince Philip, at the age of nine, signed this photograph of himself in Greek national costume for his nanny, 'Roosie', Miss Emily Roose.

67. A smiling Prince Philip as an attendant lord, Donalbain, in the Gordonstoun
School production of *Macbeth*, July 1935.

His skill as an artist and his appreciation for the arts stem from his time at the
Elms.

Although not remembered for his academic record, Philip's prowess at games
was memorable, for it was there that his true competitive nature and extrovert
character came out to the full in team and individual sports. When he left,
Catherine Pegg wrote, 'When the time came for him to go to his English school
we were, teachers and school fellows all, sorry to part with our tried and trusted
democratic little friend whom we all had known as "Just Philip".'

At this time Philip's parents slowly began to drift apart. Prince Andrew could not forgive or forget his savage treatment and humilation by his people and his family began to find him ' . . . intractable, his equanimity in tatters'. When not in a state of depression, he was a 'tall, genial, smiling gentleman, . . . a man of the world' who found solace, despite his reduced means, in Parisian society. By contrast, Princess Alice turned more and more to religion and charitable pursuits. She had set up a shop called 'Hellas' in the Faubourg St Honoré. There, she sold Greek embroidery, tapestries and medallions, the proceeds going to help Greek refugees.

Amidst this split, the question of Philip's education was discussed. Prince Andrew and the daughters were strongly pro-German while Princess Alice and her Mountbatten brothers naturally favoured England as the most suitable place to educate Philip. The final break-up of the family came in 1930, when Philip was nine and the first of the daughters, Sophie, aged just sixteen, married her Hesse cousin. The three other sisters all married German cousins within the next year and their parents, seeing their parental duty fulfilled, finally parted. Prince Andrew went to live at his sister-in-law's family Casino in Monte Carlo and Princess Alice finally returned to Athens. She first took Philip to England and left him with her mother, the Marchioness of Milford Haven, at Kensington Palace. When the 'rugged, boisterous boy' found the Palace too constricting, her brother George, Marquess of Milford Haven, who had been appointed his guardian, took him to live with his family at Lynden Manor. From then on, Philip's life was inextricably bound to the Mountbattens in England, although there were still occasional visits to his mother in Athens and Corfu.

It was Lord Milford Haven who suggested Cheam School for Philip. His own father, when First Sea Lord, had been impressed by the confidence displayed by two of his midshipmen, and had asked where they went to school. On learning that it was Cheam, he decided that that was the school for his son George. George in turn sent his son, David, there and he was joined by Philip for the summer term of 1930.

Cheam, one of the oldest preparatory schools in the country, was established in the little Surrey village near Sutton in 1695. David and Philip were among the last pupils to the school before it was moved from the suburbs to the Berkshire Downs. Philip was lucky to have the company of David, two years his senior, as it cushioned the blow of leaving his family, and soon, with his extrovert character, he was thriving amongst the boys of his own age, and enjoying school life.

Discipline was strict among the ninety or so boys and their surroundings were austere. In common with most preparatory schools, the beds were hard, dormitories draughty with bare floors full of splinters. As at the Elms, Philip excelled more on the games field than the classroom. He captained the soccer team in his final year and was a good athlete and swimmer. History was his best subject after French for which he won a prize—hardly surprising since he had lived in France for seven years.

Both Philip and David were keen Boy Scouts and one summer they rode their bicycles from Maidenhead to a Scout camp at Dover. Seeking an easier return, they hitched a lift on a Thames grain barge to London, for two days and nights, sleeping on the sacks of grain, 'thrilled by all the sights and sounds of the sea'.

While Lord Louis Mountbatten, Philip's younger uncle, was a great influence on his nephew, he was a serving naval officer and away for much of the time. Philip's real mentor during those impressionable early years, was his guardian. In true Mountbatten tradition, Lord Milford Haven had served in the Royal Navy rising to the rank of Captain. He had fought during the War with great valour and he frequently regaled the boys with stories of Jutland and Heligoland. Although he resigned his commission for the more lucrative rewards of commerce, to finance his house and family, it was mainly he who influenced the young Philip towards a career in the Royal Navy.

Despite these thoroughly English aspects of his life, Philip was to go to Germany for the next phase of his education. His sister, Theodora, had married Bertold, Margrave of Baden, whose father Prince Max, the last Chancellor of Imperial Germany, had retired after the First World War to his estates and castles of Salem on the forested shores of Lake Constance, where he had established a revolutionary type of school in a wing of his vast Schloss. His aim was to create a new élite and he combined the basic British public-school system with the thoroughness of German teaching. He started the school for Bertold and three other pupils, but when it grew, he brought in his friend and adviser, Dr Kurt Hahn, as headmaster in 1920. By the time Philip arrived in the winter term of 1932 it was the foremost school in Europe with 400 pupils. Philip remained for only three terms, for he disliked being taken from his pleasant, carefree existence in England and set down in the humourless, spartan atmosphere of Salem. He did not excel. Games, usually his strong point, were considered unimportant and he muddled through his studies. The emphasis was 'not to turn out tame deer but to give the boys opportunities for self-discovery' and 'to free the sons of the wealthy and powerful from an enervating sense of privilege.'

It was not long after Philip's arrival that the liberal ideas of Salem clashed with those of Nazism and the headmaster, Kurt Hahn, was arrested. He was released through the intervention of Prince Bertold and he escaped to England. The Brownshirts, with their ridiculous salutes and heel-clicking and beliefs, were anathema to Philip and he openly mocked them when they paraded in the town. Once, he asked an SS officer with his arm outstretched in a Nazi salute if he wanted to go to the lavatory, then roared with laughter. Prince Bertold thought it safer that he, Theodora and Philip should follow Dr Hahn to England and so Philip returned to the care of his uncle.

Philip was one of the thirty pupils who now joined Dr Hahn's new school of Gordonstoun. At Salem, Philip had been unhappy and unco-operative but he now thrived under the new régime. He worked his way up through the school, ending up as 'guardian' or head-boy. When he left, Hahn wrote: 'Prince Philip is universally trusted, liked, and respected. He had the greatest sense of service of all the boys in the school. Prince Philip's leadership qualities are most

68. Prince Philip, captain of the first XI cricket team, going in to bat for
Gordonstoun, 1938.

69. Members of the Royal Family on a balcony during the visit of King George VI and Queen Elizabeth to the Royal College, Dartmouth, on July 22 1939. It was the first time that Princess Elizabeth, second left, had met Prince Philip, just visible next to the King.

noticeable, though marred at times by impatience and intolerance. He will need the exacting demand of a great service to do justice to himself. His best is outstanding; his second best is not good enough. Prince Philip will make his mark in any profession where he will have to prove himself in a full trial of strength.'

Undoubtedly, Philip has made the most of an unusual upbringing and childhood. His personality and strength of character helped him cope with the difficulties of being a displaced royal and with the wanderings of his childhood, from country to country, from school to school and from parents to guardians. The experience left him neither bitter nor reproachful as he turned those trials to his advantage and he has proved himself, as Hahn predicted, as a resolute husband, father and Prince consort.

6

Anne

Monday, 15 August 1950 was a particularly hot and sunny day. There was an air of expectancy in London and a large crowd of well-wishers had formed outside Clarence House waiting for news from within. At a little after mid-day, the news came that Princess Elizabeth and the Duke of Edinburgh had had a daughter and a great cheer went up outside the house. The news was thought so important that play was stopped at the Oval Cricket Ground (part of the Prince of Wales's Kennington estates) and over the loudspeakers came the announcement, 'Ladies and Gentlemen—we have a new baby Princess.' If Londoners had not heard the news, they certainly heard the two forty-one-gun salutes from the Tower of London and from the guns of the King's Troop, Royal Horse Artillery, in Hyde Park.

According to the bulletin posted outside the railings of Clarence House:

Her Royal Highness The Princess Elizabeth, Duchess of Edinburgh, was safely delivered of a Princess at 11.50 am today. Her Royal Highness and her daughter are both doing well.
William Gilliat, John H. Peel, Vernon F. Hall, John Weir.

The Queen, who had arrived shortly before the birth, declared, 'It's a lovely baby!' Inside the Palace, Princess Elizabeth was thrilled to have produced first a son, then, twenty-one months later, a daughter. Prince Philip was doubly pleased for earlier that same day he had heard that he had been gazzetted Lieutenant-Commander and been appointed to his first command, HMS *Magpie*, a frigate with the Mediterranean Fleet. He telephoned his mother, Princess Alice, who was staying with his grandmother, the Marchioness of Milford Haven, at Kensington Palace, and described the baby as 'the sweetest girl'. As the baby was late in arriving the Queen knew that the King would only fret in London, so she sent him ahead to Balmoral. The news was telephoned through, but the King was on the moors and it took a gillie nearly an hour to find him. Later, when he went to Balmoral to ask permission to call the baby Anne Elizabeth Alice Louise, Prince Philip told the King himself of the birth of the six-pound baby with her mass of dark hair. Permission for the names was readily given, the King finding

70. Princess Anne, nearly one, in the arms of her mother, Princess Elizabeth, with her father, Prince Philip, holding Prince Charles in the grounds of their first country home, Windlesham Moor, Berkshire, 1951.

them 'unusual and charming'. Another filial duty for Prince Philip was to register the birth of his daughter with the Westminster Registry Office, whereupon she was issued with an identity card, number MAPM3/96, and a child's ration book, a reminder of the restrictions of the Second World War that were still in force.

For the first few weeks, Anne slept in a cot in her mother's dressing room and the Clarence House staff took it in turns to file past and inspect the baby. The public had to wait for their first sight of the baby until Cecil Beaton, the Court photographer, was called to take pictures of mother and daughter. Later, Beaton recalled 'a small baby with quite a definite nose for one so young, large, sleepy grey-green eyes and a particularly pretty mouth.'

After a brief spell in Scotland, the Royal Family were united in London for Anne's christening. The chosen names of Anne Elizabeth Alice Louise were a mixture from both sides of the family and from three of her sponsors—Elizabeth and Alice after the grandmothers, and Louise after 'Uncle Dicky' Mountbatten whose Christian name was Louis. Anne was chosen simply because her parents liked the name rather than because of any throwback to the house of Stuart. The other sponsors were her aunt, Princess Margarita of Hohenlohe-Langengberg, and her cousin, the Honourable Andrew Elphinstone. Following in her brother Charles's footsteps, she was christened in the Music Room, wearing the traditional Honiton Lace christening robes and was baptised in the Golden Lily Font with water from the River Jordan. The Archbishop of York, Dr Cyril Garbett, officiated and Anne behaved impeccably throughout the ceremony.

While Princess Elizabeth was given nearly 'a year off' to care for the baby Charles, she continued with her busy schedule, taking the pressure off her frail father, soon after her daughter was born. Thus Anne was left in the care of the nursery staff, headed by Mrs Lightbody. In the nursery, it was the same routine for Anne as for Charles, the accent being on plenty of fresh air, with rests in the garden of Clarence House, and walks in St James's Park opposite. As so often the case with the younger child catching up with the older, Anne developed quickly. Despite her royal duties, Princess Elizabeth was still the wife of a serving naval officer and she joined her husband in Malta for that Christmas of 1950. Shortly after Anne's first birthday, her parents embarked on a tour of Canada and the United States of America and preparations were being made for their Commonwealth Tour of Australia and New Zealand in January of 1952. Despite these long, forced absences, during which Charles and Anne went to Buckingham Palace to stay with their grandparents, they grew into a close-knit and loving family.

When Anne was eighteenth months old, King George VI died, on 6 February 1952, and her family moved to Buckingham Palace. On the accession of her mother as Queen, Anne became the second in line to the throne and fourth woman in the realm, facts that were to be hidden from her for as long as possible in the new Queen's efforts to give her children as normal an upbringing as possible. One departure from custom was that neither she nor Charles should curtsey or bow to their parents, though it was upheld for the old Queen Mary. Anne, showing early on the independent side of her nature, refused to curtsey, as she 'shyly hung her head, scuffed the carpet with her shoe and looked vague'. Considered far too young to attend the Coronation in 1953, she was left behind to watch the ceremony and processions on television and fumed at her brother who was allowed to attend part of the service.

Anne grew into an enchanting-looking child with a mass of fair curls, blue eyes like her mother and a rosy complexion. Despite her gentle looks she was a tough child, preferring tomboy pursuits like climbing trees to playing with dolls. She was cleverer than her brother with her hands, being adept at modelling with plasticine or making up plastic model kits with her father. She

71. Princess Anne with her mother, being photographed by Prince Charles, at Balmoral, 1952.

was also quick-witted and enjoyed card games that had an element of skill and jigsaw puzzles. Best of all, perhaps, were the rocking horse inherited from her mother and her brother's mechanical pony and trap which she pedalled all over the long corridors of Buckingham Palace. The inanimate horses were soon replaced by a real pony, a strawberry roan called William, which Anne shared with her brother.

The Queen and Prince Philip made every effort not to favour either child, but with Charles being the elder, a boy and heir to the throne, it was difficult for Anne not to feel less important. This subconscious distancing sometimes resulted in her making herself felt in other ways, such as tantrums in the nursery or the rebellion against Nanny Lightbody's strict régime. Occasionally she became moody, but never for long. In the main, however, Anne was bright, alert and always very energetic, and in that way her character has often been compared to that of her forthright father.

The personalities of the Queen's two children were totally different. Whereas Charles tended to shrink into his shell when in public, Anne would be the one to wave and show herself off. It was she who would climb around the battlements of Windsor Castle or feed biscuits to the Russian brown bear, Niki—a present from the Soviet leaders Khruschev and Bulganin. A favourite ploy of hers was to walk past the sentries at Buckingham Palace and Windsor Castle to make them present arms to her. By contrast, Charles would go out of his way to avoid the salute.

From birth, brother and sister spent practically all their time with adults, either their nannies, or their parents whom they saw every morning and at tea and bathtime and during the weekends and holidays at Balmoral and Sandringham, or their parents' friends. As a result, Anne was totally at ease with older people and, by her own admission, she disliked other little girls, and fought with the boys, so 'wasn't a very popular person'.

When Charles graduated to the schoolroom for lessons with Miss Peebles, Anne was left in the nursery with Mabel Anderson. With only one child in the nursery, two nannies were superfluous and 'by an amicable agreement' Nanny Lightbody left the royal nursery. Mabel Anderson was certainly Anne's favourite nanny. She had slept in her room since she was a baby and a close bond of affection grew between them. Mabel Anderson was to stay at Buckingham Palace to care for the Queen and Prince Philip's next two children, Andrew and Edward.

When she was five, Anne started in the schoolroom with Miss Peebles, 'Mispy' to Charles but 'Bambi' to Anne. Her early lessons were very much the same as her brother's with classes in the mornings and educational visits to places of interest in the afternoon. Unlike her brother, who by that time had gone away to Cheam School, it was thought that it would be beneficial to have other girls to share the schoolroom. In May 1957, two girls were chosen to do their lessons with Anne: Caroline Hamilton who was the grand-daughter of the Dean of Windsor, and Susan Babington-Smith, known as Suki, who was the

72. Princess Anne with her great-aunt, The Princess Royal, watching the Trooping of the Colour from the balcony of Buckingham Palace, June 1957.

73. The Queen and Princess Anne with her pony, William, at Windsor, December 1959.

grand-daughter of Admiral the Honourable Sir Herbert Meade-Featherstonehaugh, a former equerry to King George V and Commander of the Royal Yachts. Lessons varied little from the old routine except that three unknown little girls out with their Governess attracted much less attention than had the familiar face of Charles. Consequently, they had greater freedom from the press for their educational visits in the afternoon.

Miss Peebles's lessons were supplemented by others from outside. Piano was taught by Miss Hilda Bor and weekly French lessons were taken by a Mademoiselle Susanne Josseron at Buckingham Palace and by a young French-Canadian, Lieutenant Jean Lajeunesse, who went to Balmoral for a month's conversation in the summer holidays. Much more important to Anne than the schoolroom were her outdoor activities. Her father took her sailing, to begin with on Loch Muick, near Balmoral, then when she was a little older, she accompanied him on his yacht *Bloodhound* on their summer cruises. Skating was another pastime and Anne and her two companions, Caroline and Suki, went to Richmond ice-rink for lessons. The instructor found Anne's 'fearless' approach quite remarkable.

As Princess Anne entered the Royal Box during the 1981 Wimbledon Lawn Tennis Championships, the commentator, Dan Maskell, recalled his days as the tennis coach at Buckingham Palace. In his opinion, if Anne had not concentrated on horses, she could have been a top-class tennis player. Horses, however, have played a much more important part in Anne's life and, entirely through ability, she became the three-day event European Champion in 1971 and represented Great Britain in the 1976 Montreal Olympics. From the humble beginnings of William, her roan, she rode a mare called Greensleeves, then, when she was taught by Mrs Sybil Smith, she was given a mare called Mayflower. There was a great precedent for Anne to ride well, for her mother was an accomplished horsewoman and her father a rising polo player. With Windsor Great Park to ride in and the Royal Mews full of horses for her to ride, there was every opportunity for her to become really proficient.

One of the great Buckingham Palace institutions was the Brownie and Girl Guide packs and at Princess Margaret's suggestion, the 'Bham Palace' troop was resurrected. Much was made of the fact that the daughters of an electrician and a taxi-driver were in Anne's Company but in reality, the Brownies were drawn from privileged backgrounds. It did, however, widen Anne's circle of friends and it suited her forceful character and practical nature. Later, when she graduated to the Girl Guides, the guide officers found her thoughtful but fun-loving and rather noisy.

The first half of 1960 was a particularly exciting time for Anne. She began the year by acting as chief bridesmaid to her cousin, Pamela Mountbatten, when she married David Hicks, an interior decorator. The next excitement was to be taken by her father to see her new brother, Andrew, just an hour after he was born on 19 February. The biggest excitement of all, perhaps, was the wedding of her aunt, Princess Margaret, to Antony Armstrong-Jones. Again, Anne was the chief bridesmaid of the eight little girls at the ceremony held in Westminster Abbey on 6 May. Anne was much in demand as a bridesmaid the next year, too; on 8 June 1961 she was chief bridesmaid to a cousin, the Duke of Kent, when he married Miss Katherine Worsley. One of her 'charges' was the four-year-old Jane Spencer, goddaughter of the bridegroom and sister of the present Princess of Wales, who was born twelve days later.

By the time Anne was twelve, it was becoming increasingly clear that she and her two friends were outgrowing the schoolroom and Miss Peebles' régime. Her parents asked her if she would like to go to a boarding school. She replied that she would, but ruefully admitted later that the end result would have been little different if she had said 'no'. Apart from its academic record and pleasant staff and surroundings, Benenden was chosen for Anne for its proximity to various

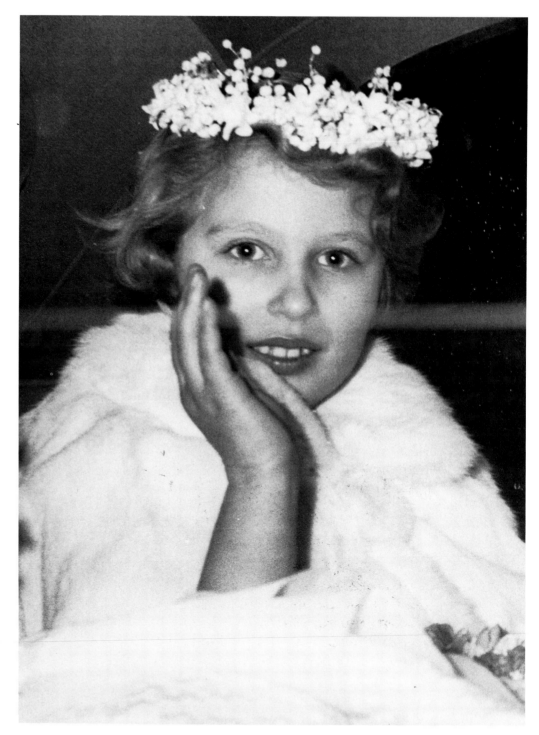

74. Princess Anne leaving the reception at Romsey Abbey where she was a bridesmaid to her cousin, Lady Pamela Mountbatten, in January 1960.

friends and relations of the Royal Family whom she could visit over the weekends. The school is in the Weald of Kent, not that far from London but just remote enough to put off the press photographers.

Consciously looking forward to her new experience, Anne came south from Balmoral with her mother for the first day of the Michaelmas term 1963, shortly after her thirteenth birthday. She arrived at Benenden to find that the whole of the staff, under the headmistress Miss E. B. Clarke, and the entire school of nearly 230 pupils, had lined up outside the Victorian house to meet her. This was to be the only recognition that the Queen's daughter was at the school and, thereafter, Anne was treated like any other pupil.

Benenden has an admirable system of introducing new girls to the complexities of school-life by way of a 'house mother', usually a girl in her second term. Anne, with her independent and outward nature, and with the help of her house mother, soon settled into the school and adapted well to the strange life. True to her character, she never remembered being homesick. To some, the rules of a boarding-school are an unwanted restriction but to Anne, her time at Benenden provided a new-found liberty. Just to be an ordinary girl amongst others was freedom enough.

Anne enjoyed her time at Benenden, behaving like any other high-spirited schoolgirl. Occasionally, she would hold back on some prank or action if she consciously thought it would reflect badly on her parents or embarrass them in any way. She was certainly not the dim pupil the press branded her (and her brother Charles). She left with six 'O' levels and two 'A' levels in history and geography. By her own admission she did not work as hard as she could have and her headmistress put the adequate, but not good grades of her 'A' levels down to 'possessing far more academic ability than she cared to exercise, and working at school only as hard as was strictly necessary.'

Throughout her time at Benenden, Anne was always extremely physically fit. She enjoyed games and, unlike Charles at Gordonstoun, did well in team sports. She played netball and lacrosse and was in the school team for the Schools' Lacrosse Tournament in 1968 where she remained unrecognised throughout. The early coaching from Dan Maskell gave Anne a good grounding in tennis and she made the House team, although she admits that she 'kind of fell to pieces' when the competition became too intense. These sporting activities, although important to Anne, were secondary to her riding. Like other girls at Benenden, she was allowed to keep her own pony, High Jinks, at a nearby livery stable and was able to continue her riding lessons twice a week. It was that careful and expert early tuition that stood her in such good stead throughout her riding career. Today, she admits 'It's the one thing I can do well and can be seen to do well.'

From early childhood, Anne never failed to show her mettle. Like her father, she has always shown a forthright approach to life and to her royal duties, a trait in both of them which has not always endeared them to the public or the press. But her critics have not, or have deliberately tried not to understand the complexities of her character when set against her royal background. In some

75. The first day of term, September 1963, at Benenden. The Queen is talking to the headmistress, Miss Clarke, while Princess Anne meets her housemistress, Miss Gee.

ways, Anne is more 'royal' in a historical sense than any of her relations, making the monarchy fit her lifestyle rather than the other way round. It is also her independent manner, that of a girl who enjoys her own company, coupled with a rich Hanoverian temper, that makes her different from her family, making her appear more alive than her brothers. Throughout her formative years, she has had all the competitiveness of a second child. It is that spirit and desire to win which is as apparent today as it was when she was a child.

7

Andrew and Edward

According to Prince Philip, 'People want their first child very much. They want their second almost as much. If a third comes along they accept it as natural, even if they haven't gone out of their way to try for it.' This was certainly true of his and the Queen's third child, Andrew. The baby can hardly have been 'planned' because the critical second and third months of the Queen's pregnancy coincided with an exhaustive tour of Canada and the United States in the summer of 1959. Against all advice, the Queen insisted that the tour go ahead and she only took the precaution of taking an extra seamstress with her to let out her clothes. In the end, the tour went well and only one town was disappointed that it was visited by Prince Philip on his own. The Queen returned to England tired and exhausted and went to Balmoral soon after to rest and relax in the bracing Scottish air for the remainder of the summer.

Remembering only too well the noise in the Mall after Charles's birth, the Queen chose for her confinement the Belgian Suite in Buckingham Palace overlooking the gardens and the lake beyond. The large bathroom was converted into the delivery room and the Queen moved down from her apartments the day before the baby was due. At 3.30 the next afternoon, 19 February 1960, the baby was born. It was an easy delivery and not long after, the royal midwife, Sister Helen Rowe, showed the proud father his 7 lb 3 oz son. As at the births of his two elder children, Charles and Anne, Prince Philip had ordered the Palace refrigerators to be filled with champagne to toast the health of the baby and he gave a bouquet of white roses and carnations to his wife.

The usual excitement still followed this latest royal birth—crowds in the Mall, the twenty-one gun salutes, the loyal messages of Parliament, the flags and the bunting—but in addition, for the new infant Prince, there was a fly-past of the Black Arrows, made up of thirty-six Hunter jets, over Buckingham Palace.

The Queen and Prince Philip had been married for twelve-and-a-half years. They had always wanted a larger family, not only because they liked children, but also to make the monarchy even more secure. The birth of Andrew, and four years later of Edward, doubly assured their dynasty, at least for the next generation.

76. Prince Andrew, aged six months, being carried by his nanny, Mabel Anderson, before boarding the train to Scotland at the start of the Balmoral summer holiday, 1960.

The new Prince was christened Andrew Albert Christian Edward, the names of his grandfathers and great-great-grandfathers, Kings Edward VII and Christian IX of Denmark. He was also the first royal child to be styled by the surname of the Royal Family, Mountbatten-Windsor. Shortly before Andrew was born, the Queen, in recognition of the invaluable service of Prince Philip as consort and as head of their family, ordained that 'While I and my children shall continue to be styled and known as the House and family of Windsor, my descendants shall bear the name of Mountbatten-Windsor.' When Princess Anne married she used that surname but when the Prince of Wales married, he just signed the marriage register, 'Charles P'.

During their early years, the Queen had indulged the public clamour for news, photographs and appearances of Charles and Anne. As a result, they had become cult figures and were considered public property. In retrospect, the Queen and Prince Philip realised that they had made mistakes in giving way to public demand, and they resolved that their third son would be shielded from all such pressures. When Andrew was born, the Queen had reigned for eight years. With the help of her husband, she had mastered the complexities of her job, she was competent and efficient. Above all, she had the confidence and experience to divide her time between affairs of State and her family. Those early demands on her as Queen had robbed her of much of the pleasures of motherhood of her two eldest children and she was determined that she was not going to be similarly deprived with her third baby. The same was true of Prince Philip. The Queen as Sovereign takes precedence over her husband but Prince Philip is unquestionably head of his family. He cares deeply for his children and has always been ready to guide them through any difficulty. He has encouraged them in every area where they showed talent or interest. If he was strict with his children it was because he fully realised that any lapse in effort or loss of standard would cause problems for them later.

The protective part of Andrew's early life began immediately. Cecil Beaton took the first official photographs of mother and baby and then the Buckingham Palace wall of silence came down. Andrew appeared in official photographs to mark the Queen Mother's sixtieth birthday, but with little else to seize upon, the Continental newspapers began, typically, to speculate that the baby was deformed. For those who knew, however, he was a healthy baby with blue eyes and very fair hair, who rarely cried.

With his mother's influence, Andrew's nursery routine was considerably relaxed compared to that of Charles and Anne. The strict régime of Nanny Lightbody had given way to the benign Mabel Anderson, 'Mamba' to Andrew. She was delighted to have another baby in the royal nursery since Charles, eleven years old, was away at his preparatory school and Anne, nine-and-a-half years old, spent much of her time with her governess, Miss Peebles. Miss Anderson could concentrate on Andrew, while an under-nanny, June Waller, was taken on to care for Anne. As with the two elder children, Andrew was brought down to see his parents in their bedrooms in the morning and they,

77. A reluctant corgi being coaxed off the train by Prince Andrew, watched by the
Queen and Prince Edward, January 1966.

78. Bill Anderson, a 19-stone shot-putter, dwarfs the Duke of Edinburgh, the Queen Mother, Princess Margaret, Prince Andrew and David Lindley at the Braemar Gathering, September 1967.

when their public duties allowed, went up to the nursery for tea and bathtime. It is certainly true that the Queen and Prince Philip devoted more time to Andrew in his early years than they had been able to give to Charles and Anne. On Nanny Anderson's days off, the Queen would take personal charge of the nursery. When Andrew—and, later, Edward—were slightly older, they were allowed to play in the Queen's sitting room while she worked on her 'Boxes' (official correspondence). It had been the one room out-of-bounds to Charles and Anne.

When Anne left for her boarding school, Benenden, at the end of 1963, Andrew was left in the nursery on his own. He was not to enjoy the sole attention of his parents and nursery staff for long because, on 10 March 1964 at 8.20 am, his brother, Edward, was born. He was born five days earlier than expected which was fortunate in one sense as his father had to leave soon after for the funeral of his cousin, King Paul of Greece. On his return, his youngest son was christened Edward Antony Richard Louis—Antony after his uncle, Lord Snowdon, and Richard after his cousin, the young Duke of Gloucester. The

Queen and Prince Philip's family was now complete and, despite the wide spread of over fifteen years between the children, they have always been the greatest friends and thoroughly enjoy each other's company.

From the earliest age, Andrew has shown an extrovert and mischievous character, an inquiring mind, even an obstinate streak, all mixed with great charm. He emulated both his father and his sister, Anne, when they were in public, by waving to the crowd or shaking hands with the lines of dignitaries waiting to meet them. He adored his father and always tried hardest in his company.

For Andrew, the days of uninterrupted play were over when he reached the age of five. The Queen had already taught him to read and count, but it was now time for him to have proper lessons. Miss Katherine Peebles, Charles and Anne's governess, was brought back, and a class was made up of Andrew's contemporaries—two boys, Justin Beaumont and James Steel, and two girls, Katie Seymour and the Honourable Victoria Butler, all of them the children or grandchildren of members or ex-members of Royal Households. Andrew flourished at his lessons, once his governess managed to curb his unruly behaviour, and showed a flair that was never there with his elder brother. Like Anne with her Brownies, Andrew and, later, Edward, were to widen their circle of aquaintances when they joined the 1st Marylebone Cub Pack. Each week, a mini-bus would deliver the other cubs to Buckingham Palace and out would clamber a cosmopolitan group, among them the sons of tradespeople, of a policeman and of a Pakistani immigrant.

Despite the four years that separate the brothers, Andrew and Edward have always been close. Yet they have very different characters. Where Andrew was noisy and active, Edward tended to be more like his older brother, quieter and artistic, although not as shy and retiring. The Royal Family are renowned for their love of practical jokes and Andrew eagerly followed in that vein. Where Anne delighted in making the sentries present arms to her, Andrew derived considerable amusement in tying their bootlaces together as they stood, immobile, to attention. The Royal Family strongly suspected that it was he who once poured 'bubble-bath' into the swimming pool at Windsor, and caused chaos by turning the signs round directing the guests at a garden party at Buckingham Palace. His pranks were received with mixed feelings and his mother diplomatically said of him that 'he was not always a little ray of sunshine'.

Just as Edward was catching up his brother and eligible for the school-room, his brother left to go to his preparatory school, Heatherdown, near Ascot in Berkshire, starting in the Michaelmas term of 1969. It was no longer a novelty for the Queen's children to go to private schools and Andrew fitted into the school with the minimum of fuss. At the same time, Edward started his lessons in the schoolroom at Buckingham Palace. The faithful governess, Miss Peebles, died shortly after Andrew had left and she was replaced by Lavinia Keppel, of the same family as Mrs Alice Keppel, the mistress of King Edward VII. Edward

79. Prince Andrew and his cousins, David Lindley and Sarah Armstrong-Jones, with the Queen, Queen Mother and Princess Anne at Windsor Great Park, April 1968.

joined, among others, his cousins, David and Sarah Armstrong-Jones, Princess Margaret's children, the Duke and Duchess of Kent's eldest son, George (Earl of St Andrews), and Princess Alexandra and Angus Ogilvy's son, James. It was a happy class and the friendships formed there are as strong today as they were then.

Andrew greatly enjoyed his preparatory school. Whereas Charles was miserable when he first went to Cheam, Andrew took to Heatherdown immediately. Not only did he make friends easily, he became the 'natural boss' his father had predicted. At the Queen's insistence, he was treated like any other boy except that he had a Special Branch officer shadowing him everywhere. The security was in fact necessary. By the spring of 1971, Andrew had been joined at Heatherdown by his cousin, George St Andrews, and, not long after, the police uncovered an IRA plot to kidnap the young Earl as a hostage for the release of two convicted terrorists. When term started, the school was kept under surveillance by the Special Branch until the threat passed.

80. Prince Edward with his cousins, David Lindley and Sarah Armstrong-Jones, watch the arrival of the Black Watch Regiment at Balmoral, August 1968.

81. Andrew still has time to stick his tongue out at the camera during his last meeting with the 1st St Marylebone Cubs, 1968.

The school holidays for Andrew, and later Edward, were a constant source of fun and outdoor activity. Their father taught them to shoot, swim and sail while the Queen Mother inspired them to learn how to cast a fly for salmon and trout on her stretch of water at Birkhall, her house on the Balmoral estate. With the spate of royal babies and marriages in the early 1960s, the Queen decided that Sandringham would be too cramped for their traditional Royal Christmas and so the venue was moved to Windsor. After Christmas, the children and a few cousins resumed their holiday at Sandringham. Andrew and Edward particularly liked those holidays for the shoots and the rounds of children's parties, not least those given by Lord Althorp at Park House, within the grounds of Sandringham, for his youngest children, Diana and Charles Spencer.

As a result of Andrew's successful experience at Heatherdown, the Queen and

Prince Philip decided that it was safe to send Edward to a day-preparatory school in London. His cousin, James Ogilvy, was sent to his father's old preparatory school, Gibbs in Kensington, and Edward joined him, aged seven-and-a-half, for the Michaelmas term 1971. He was a sensitive boy, quiet and with good manners and he settled into the school without the rumpus that accompanied his eldest brother, Charles. Occasionally, his exalted background came out. During an art class, the pupils were asked to draw a house. Among the pile of modest town houses and cottages was an enormous palace with sentries and standards, with the name 'Edward' in the corner.

During a television interview, Prince Philip discussed his policy of privacy for his two youngest sons by saying, 'You cannot have it both ways. We try to keep the children out of the public eye so that they can grow up as normal as possible. But if you are going to have a monarchy you have got to have a family, and the family's got to be in the public eye.' The exposure of his younger sons to public gaze had so far been minimal, although they had been seen in the film of a picnic at Balmoral during the Queen's Christmas message of 1969 and again in the drawing-room of Sandringham turning the pages of a photograph album for the 1971 Christmas message.

The brothers were to overlap at Heatherdown for a year before Andrew went on to Gordonstoun. The school was relieved to see him go for they had occasionally found their royal pupil difficult. For most of the time he was diligent, studious, active and polite, but he would also descend into black moods and become morose and ill-mannered. Despite being a new boy, Andrew adopted an air of self-importance, but it impressed no one and the other pupils saw through it. They either ignored him or teased him by mimicking his pomposity.

There had been enormous changes to Gordonstoun in the six years between the time that Charles left and Andrew arrived. Although the aims of the school were the same, the new headmaster, John Kempe, had made sweeping changes. The bare boards, chill, draughty dormitories, cold showers and Spartan life of Philip's and Charles's days had been replaced by altogether more comfortable surroundings and a much more relaxed régime. The educational standards had also improved and the accent had moved from individual sports to team games like rugger. However, the greatest innovation at Gordonstoun was the admission of girls to the school.

Whatever the pupils of Gordonstoun thought of Andrew that first term, they can only have been impressed when an Andover of the Queen's Flight was sent to collect him for the wedding of his sister, Anne, to Captain Mark Phillips on 14 November 1973. It was an even bigger day for Edward since his sister had chosen him as her page, the only bridesmaid being their cousin, Sarah Armstrong-Jones. For both boys, it was their first major public function and they travelled to Westminster Abbey together in a State Landau in the bride's carriage procession. For an eight-year-old boy, Edward managed the ordeal well and earned high praise.

82. Miss Lavinia Keppel in the schoolroom at Buckingham Palace with three of her pupils, Prince Edward (right), Sarah Armstrong-Jones and James Faber.

Once Andrew had settled down at Gordonstoun, he did well, not only academically but on the sports field. He played good football and cricket and was a keen tennis and squash player as well. With his extrovert character, he soon won himself a place as a leader and, as a master observed, he had 'no time for sycophants and if anyone tries to take the mickey out of him, he fights back. He's just as good with his verbalistics as with his fists.' To many, but by no means all, of the girls at Gordonstoun he was irresistible. This considerable attention to women was due both to what his elder brother huffily called his 'Robert Redford looks' and to his enormous confidence. Another skill that was kindled at Gordonstoun was his love of flying. He began training as a glider pilot and within six months had completed the course and gained his wings after making three four-minute solo flights at Milltown Airfield not far from the school. Academically he also took and passed six 'O' levels.

The time Charles had spent in Australia at Timbertop was undoubtedly the turning-point of his life. The Queen and Prince Philip decided to repeat the experiment and arranged for Andrew to go to school in Canada for two terms. Andrew had already been to Canada with the Royal Family to watch Princess Anne compete as a member of the British Equestrian team in the Olympic Games in 1976. He had enjoyed his visit greatly and so, in January 1977, Andrew went

18. Prince Andrew was a Cub in the 1st St Marylebone Pack, seen here in the grounds of Buckingham Palace, 1968.

19. Prince Charles, holding Prince Edward, watches Prince Andrew play bagatelle in the drawing room of Sandringham, 1969.

20. Prince Edward and Lady Sarah Armstrong-Jones in Windsor Great Park, May 1971.

21. Prince Edward leading fellow-pupils of Gibbs School, London, during his first term, October 1971.

22. The royal cousins at Windsor Castle on Christmas Day, 1969. Lady Helen Windsor, leading, is followed by Princess Anne, Marina Ogilvie, the Earl of St Andrews, and Lady Sarah Armstrong-Jones, with Prince Charles in the rear.

23. The Prince and Princess of Wales at a concert of Christmas Music at their local Parish Church, St Mary's, Tetbury, Gloucestershire on 6 December 1981.

24. Royal mother—Lord Snowdon's superb portrait of the Princess of Wales on her 21st birthday, an occasion coinciding neatly with the birth of her first child.

83. The Duke of Edinburgh and his two younger sons, Princes Andrew and Edward, examine the cockpit of a helicopter at the Farnborough Air Show, September 1976.

to Lakefield School, nearly seventy miles from Toronto in Ontario. It was an ideal choice of school and he flourished in a tough, healthy atmosphere with a varied programme of lessons, sports and expeditions. Like Charles, he returned from Canada a different person. Although always full of self-confidence, now he was a more mature, thoughtful and responsible person.

When Andrew returned to Gordonstoun in the autumn for the last two years of his schooling, he went with Edward who was going for his first term. Once there, however, they had little contact as Andrew was towards the top of the school and in a different house. This separation did not unduly worry Edward who wanted to make his own way in the school. Also, for all his bravado, Andrew was not universally popular and Edward took care not to be tarred with the same brush. He felt his way carefully in the school and 'didn't ram who he was down your throat'. To begin with he had few friends and was thought of very much as 'a natural goody-goody'. Some interpreted this attitude as one of superiority but he was soon to prove himself and become totally accepted by his fellow-pupils. With his father's expert tuition, he became a good sailor and, like Andrew, showed great aptitude as a glider pilot. In dramatics, he followed his elder brother by taking the lead in two bawdy plays—'Black Comedy' by Peter Shaffer and Feydeau's 'Hotel Paradiso'—put on by his and a girl's house. These successes, and a fair academic record, did much to advance him through the Gordonstoun system of privileges to 'Helper'. Generally accepted to be the brightest of all the Queen's children, Edward has nine 'O' levels and sat for three 'A' levels in June 1982.

When Andrew left Gordonstoun at the age of nineteen in June 1979, he could feel proud of his achievement at the school. Although he did not make Guardian, like his father and brother, he, too was the 'Helper', or head of house. He did well on the sports field, playing in the First XI in cricket and hockey, and gained the coveted Duke of Edinburgh gold award. 'He worked jolly hard' during his last year and passed three 'A' levels, history, English and economic and political studies, taking the examinations, at his father's suggestion, in a *nom de plume*.

Edward makes no secret of the high regard he has for Charles and was flattered when his brother asked him to be his joint supporter, the royal equivalent of best man, with Andrew, at his wedding to Lady Diana Spencer. Andrew had already made a name for himself at the Royal Naval College at Dartmouth, as a helicopter pilot and with an endless stream of pretty girls, but the Royal Wedding showed the public for the first time that Edward, too, had grown up. He enjoyed the day enormously and was proud to escort his grandmother, the Queen Mother, to St Paul's Cathedral. At that wedding, the whole Royal Family played their part, but none more than the two brothers. They performed their function as supporters with dignity and competence. At the end, they enlivened the proceedings by tying balloons and a cardboard sign with 'Just Married' written in lipstick onto the back of the State landau that took the Prince and Princess of Wales on the first stage of their honeymoon—a gesture just like that at any other family wedding.

Now that the Prince and Princess of Wales's son is second in line to the throne, thus taking precedence over the two brothers, the chances of Andrew, even less of Edward, acceding as Sovereign must be remote. They will, however, be created Royal Dukes and in time, in that capacity, will surely serve the Country and Commonwealth for many years to come.

8

The Queen's Cousins

The response to the Silver Jubilee celebrations of King George V in 1935 showed the love and respect that the public held, not only for their King, but for the whole of the Royal Family. The Duke and Duchess of York with their two little girls, Elizabeth and Margaret, were a source of constant admiration but it was the Duke's younger brother, the Duke of Kent, the debonair Prince George and his beautiful wife, Princess Marina, who really captured the imagination of that public. But it was at those Silver Jubilee celebrations that the ever-popular Duchess of Kent was criticised for wearing a large, grey hat which hid her features from the crowd. The choice of hat, however, was not so that she could hide from the spectators but so that she could hide behind it in case she felt unwell, for she was already four months pregnant.

The Duke and Duchess of Kent's first child was born on 9 October 1935 in the house the Duke had leased, 3 Belgrave Square in London. Princess Marina's parents, Prince and Princess Nicholas of Greece, and her sister Elizabeth, were staying in the house and Sir John Simon was there, too, in his capacity as Home Secretary. Edward George Nicholas Paul Patrick, as he was later christened, was born shortly after 2 am and his father and grandmother were present at the actual birth. The usual gun salutes and messages of congratulations followed and the crowds waited all night outside the house for news of the popular princess.

Shortly after the birth, the Duchess inherited a country house, Coppins, near Iver in Buckinghamshire, and the family divided their time between their two houses. The Duke was an enthusiastic father, spending 'more time in the nursery than he did in his study'. They both loved children and were thrilled when their second baby, a girl, was born fifteen months later at their Belgrave Square home. The baby, who weighed 6 lb 8 oz, was born at 11.30 on Christmas morning, 1936 to the sounds of a cornet outside playing carols and the ringing of church bells through London. Nowhere was the birth more popular than within the Royal Family who were still reeling from the effects of the Abdication: Queen Mary recorded the birth as 'the only nice thing to have happened this year'. Six weeks later the 'Infant Princess' was christened in the private chapel at Buckingham Palace—Alexandra Helen Elizabeth Olga Christabel.

84. Prince Edward and Princess Alexandra, elder children of the Duke and Duchess of Kent, leaving their home in Belgrave Square, London for their summer holiday in Sandwich, Kent, July 1938.

Despite the enormous popularity of the Duke and Duchess of Kent, it was much easier for them to keep their children out of the public eye. Edward and Alexandra grew up as any other children, mostly at Coppins with their parents and Nanny Smith. It was only when, one day, their car crashed, taking the family on their perfectly ordinary 'bucket-and-spade' holiday to Sandwich, Kent, that the public had any idea that they had been spending seaside holidays there for years.

The Duke of Kent had been appointed Governor-General designate of Australia and was due to take up his appointment in November 1939 but the outbreak of war on 3 September of that year abrogated those plans. Edward and Alexandra were at Sandringham with Queen Mary and their parents had a hard choice in deciding what best to do with them. Both Belgrave Square and Coppins were considered unsafe from attack by German bombers so the children were sent with Queen Mary and retinue to stay with her niece and her husband, the Duke and Duchess of Beaufort, at Badminton. On the way they stopped at Althorp in Northamptonshire for lunch. There they were received by Earl and Countess Spencer, the grandparents of the present Princess of Wales, where Lady Spencer laid on rice pudding for the children in the nursery.

Edward and Alexandra, aged only four and nearly three respectively, settled into the wartime routine of Badminton with their nanny and nursery maid. Their mother remained in London and travelled down to Gloucestershire by train once a week to see her children. When they were a little older, they joined the old Queen in her private war against the ivy, helping her to pull it off buildings and trees, and in her constant search for scrap iron to help the war effort. They saw their father only briefly between his travels and tours of duty.

Within that busy schedule, the Duke made certain that he was at Coppins for the birth of his third son, Michael, on 4 July 1942. The Baroness de Stoeckl, who lived in Coppins Cottage, recorded that 'the Duke seems to love this tiny infant. Every evening, instead of sitting late as usual, he leaves the table shortly after ten o'clock and carries his youngest son to the nursery and lays him in his cot and stands watching and watching. Nannie told me that each night she discreetly leaves the room, but she can hear the Duke talking softly to him.' Edward and Alexandra came up from Badminton to Windsor Castle to see their brother and witness his christening. He was given the names Michael George Charles Franklin, the last after one of his godfathers, President Franklin D. Roosevelt.

Three weeks after the christening, the Duke of Kent left Coppins to fly to Iceland for a tour of inspection. That same night, the Duchess heard the tragic news that her husband had been killed when his plane hit a mountainside in north-west Scotland. The Prime Minister, Winston Churchill, summed up the feeling of the country with the statement that 'The loss of this gallant and handsome Prince, in the prime of his life, had been a shock and a sorrow to the people of the British Empire, standing out lamentably even in these hard days of war.' After the death of her husband, the Duchess of Kent turned to her children,

85. The Duchess of Kent holding her son, Prince Michael, after his christening flanked by the Duke of Kent, Prince Edward and Princess Alexandra, August 1942.

not only for comfort in her intense sorrow but also because she realised that she now had a double parental role.

The war years of the three children were virtually all spent at Badminton with Queen Mary. A lady-in-waiting, Lady Cynthia Colville, found Alexandra 'very pretty and extraordinarily lively, attractively mischievous, with the brightest eyes I have ever seen. She got on admirably with her grandmother, Queen Mary, who was at moments taken aback by her energy, but fascinated too, and who bore her grand-daughter's exuberance with amused fortitude.' Edward and later Michael, were fascinated, like their late father, with anything mechanical and they adored cars. Edward would make Alexandra take his little steam engine apart so that he could put it back together again.

Just before the end of the war, Edward, Alexandra and Michael returned to their mother at Coppins. Although financially strained, the Duchess managed to provide a secure and happy home. It was a great blow for Alexandra when Edward was sent off to Ludgate, a preparatory school near Wokingham in Surrey, and she was left behind to continue at her 'dame school' run by a Mrs Parnell. Later, Miss Katherine Peebles, the same 'Mispy' who taught Charles, Anne and Andrew, was engaged to teach Alexandra and Michael.

The Duchess of Kent made absolutely certain that Edward, Alexandra and Michael had every opportunity of growing up as ordinary children, and because of this freedom, they became unselfconscious, quick and natural, with good manners. The three children led a more normal life than any of their royal predecessors. For their holidays they went to Balmoral, Sandringham and Windsor with their cousins, but their private family holidays were spent either at inexpensive hotels in resorts on the south coast of England or else in the Channel Islands. Edward, followed by Michael seven years later, went off to Eton, and Alexandra, at the suggestion of King George VI, went to Heathfield. Today, Princess Alexandra, with her warm smile and friendly approach, is one of the most popular members of the Royal Family—a sure reflection on her, and her brothers, sensible, uncomplicated and loving childhood.

When Michael went to Eton in 1955, he joined his cousin William, the elder son of the Duke and Duchess of Gloucester. Prince Henry, Duke of Gloucester, had married the Lady Alice Montagu-Douglas-Scott in 1935 when he was thirty-five and she a year younger, and like Alexandra, her birthday is on Christmas Day. Their long-awaited first child was born six years later, when the Duchess was practically forty and she recorded his birth and early childhood in her own words:

On December 18th 1941 William arrived, not at our home at Barnwell [Northamptonshire] as we would have wished, but at Hadley Common in Hertfordshire, a nursing home run by Almina Countess of Caernarvon, which had been evacuated from Portland Place because of the air-raids. It was conveniently near to the home of Mr Cedric Lane Roberts, the eminent gynaecologist, who had to perform the necessary Caesarean operation.

To me this was a time of great joy and thankfulness and seemed so distant from the gloom of that winter, with grave news from France and elsewhere, air raids over England and a hard cold winter on the way with snow already falling.

The Duke had been given leave from his military duties [he was on the staff of Lord Gort] to be with me for this much-longed-for event, which was to give us both such happiness. . . .

At the end of January Nana Lightbody [later nanny to Charles and Anne] arrived and stayed with the family until William and his brother outgrew their nursery days . . .

For a while life was uneventful apart from a journey to Windsor for the christening of February 22nd. This took place in the private Chapel in the Castle. Archbishop Lord Lang officiated and gave him the names of William, Henry, Andrew, Frederick, . . .

The Duke was away with the army in the Middle East and elsewhere most of that spring and summer. He wrote saying: 'I am so envious of you having William all to yourself.' It was sad for him to be parted from the baby son he was so pleased to have at last.

I took William at intervals to visit Queen Mary at Badminton; the Queen took much interest in her little grandson and was greatly amused by him.

In August the Duke and I took him to stay with my family at Drumlanrig Castle while we went onto Balmoral, and while we were there, we heard the tragic news that the Duke of Kent had been killed flying. [Thirty years later, she, too, was to receive the tragic news that William had been killed in a flying accident].

William spent the following year, 1943, mostly at Barnwell, amongst the dogs, the farm animals, his sand pit, the swimming pool, and many elderly admirers who were left to work on the farm and garden. There were more visits to Queen Mary and to Scotland and the Duchess of Kent would come to stay bringing Michael, six months younger. His father's old Nannie, Mrs Bill, would come and look after him when Nanny Lightbody went on holiday.

On 26 August 1944 the Duchess of Gloucester gave birth to William's brother, Richard Alexander Walter George. Full of excitement William went to the nursing home in Northampton to see him. With a look of dismay, he turned to Nanny Lightbody and said with indignation, 'You told me it was a little boy for me to play with and it's only a baby.' Like William, Richard was delivered by Caesarean operation.

The outbreak of the Second World War had put paid to the Duke of Kent taking up his appointment as Governor-General of Australia but that senior post was filled by his elder brother, the Duke of Gloucester. The whole family, with Nanny Lightbody in charge of William and the four-month-old Richard, left Liverpool for Australia on 16 December 1944 in great secrecy. They had a miserable journey with foul weather most of the way, a rare excitement being a German submarine which they encountered, which was sunk by their escort frigate. Once they had arrived in Australia, however, they found life at Government House in Canberra very different to the cold winter and wartime austerities of England. Richard was too young to remember much of the two years his father was Governor-General but William was three when he arrived and he enjoyed the new experience, although both children were often in poor health.

The Duke of Gloucester was brought back from Australia to help his brother, King George VI, with his heavy work load in January 1947. Back in England, William and Richard spent most of their time at the family home of Barnwell with frequent visits to their London residence, York House. Theirs was a particularly close family although their father, born in the reign of Queen Victoria and with a quick and violent temper, on occasions made their life uncomfortable at some minor misdemeanour.

Despite the increasing duties and public appearances performed by the Duke and Duchess of Gloucester as a result of his brother's ill-health, their children did not suffer from the attentions of the press like their older cousins, Elizabeth and Margaret. Consequently, they grew up exactly like any other of their landed neighbours' children, save for the few royal ceremonial occasions or holidays at Sandringham or Balmoral. William and Richard were bright little boys, both of

86. Princess Alexandra and her brother, Prince Michael, with a panda at London Zoo, May 1946.

them inventive and always active. They loved the country and had their own gardens which they tended with pride and care; William delighted in referring to his plants by their Latin names. Their uncle, the Duke of Buccleuch, was one of the biggest landowners in Britain and he fostered their love of the country and when each, in turn, inherited Barnwell, neither was a stranger to the intricacies of farming and estate management.

Before William left to go to his preparatory school, his governess, Miss Rosamond Ramirez, wrote with great foresight, 'In subjects such as literature, history, art, or wherever personal taste is important, he should do brilliantly . . . He has many good qualities: he is loyal, affectionate, idealistic and is gaining in courage and seems more patient in the face of difficulties. Much can be expected of him in the future—and for the needs of his character only the highest and the best should be demanded of him.' Of the two brothers, William was the more extrovert while Richard was quieter and artistic, a talent that he channelled into architecture as his career. From an early age, William loved anything mechanical—especially his favourite possession, a model car made and powered by a small Atco lawn mower engine.

The Duke of Gloucester was the first of his generation to go away to school and

87. Prince William of Gloucester, right, with his brother, Prince Richard, during a
county cricket match at Broadstairs, Kent, 1953.

he chose to send his sons to his old schools. His preparatory school had been absorbed by its rival, Wellesley House at Broadstairs in Kent, and William arrived there in 1950. He worked well and his marked sense of humour made him a popular figure amongst his contemporaries. He detested any form of snobbery and, like his brother who joined him at the school three years later, had little time for sychophants. They both passed into Eton, Richard with better grades than expected, and progressed through the school with no difficulty, both also passing into Cambridge University.

All who met William had foreseen a great future for the next Duke of Gloucester but, just at the time when he had proved himself in his chosen career in the Diplomatic Service, he was killed in his own aeroplane while sport-flying of 28 August 1972. His father, who had been in poor health for some time, could just comprehend the news of William's death and when he died nearly two years later, Richard succeeded to the title of Duke of Gloucester. He and his late uncle, George VI, have much in common. Both were second sons with dazzling elder brothers. Neither was trained for the role that they inherited, nor did they want it. Richard was perfectly content practising as an architect, writing his books on architecture and living his life as a 'minor royal' with the minimum of public duties. Like his uncle, he married a strong woman, the Danish Birgitte van Deurs. It is with her support and his very real sense of duty that he has succeeded in fulfilling his role as the present Duke of Gloucester.

9

The Younger Cousins

The younger members of the present Royal Family are particularly fortunate in having so many cousins of their own age. Only five years separate Andrew and Marina, the younger Ogilvy, and there are barely three months between James Ogilvy, Prince Edward, Helen Windsor (the daughter of the Duke and Duchess of Kent) and Sarah Armstrong-Jones. Throughout their lives, these cousins have all been especially close. They have done their early lessons together at Buckingham Palace, been to the same schools and they still spend part of their holidays together, especially Christmas at Windsor, Cowes Week on the Royal Yacht off the Isle of Wight or the late summers at Balmoral.

After Andrew in the hierarchy of cousins is David Armstrong-Jones, Viscount Linley of Nymans, son of Princess Margaret and the Earl of Snowdon. He was born at Clarence House, his grandmother's home, on 3 November 1961. From a very early age, he has looked identical to his father and today he has taken after him by pursuing an artistic career instead of following his elder cousins into one of the services. He, and his sister, Sarah, born on May Day 1964, had a happy childhood at Kensington Palace under the care of Nanny Sumner. Brother and sister grew up very much under the shadow of Buckingham Palace but they enjoyed the comparative freedom that Andrew and Edward had from the attentions of the press and the public eye. Princess Margaret said of them: 'My children are not Royal, they just happen to have the Queen for an aunt.' At the age of five, David joined the schoolroom at Buckingham Palace under Miss Katherine Peebles and Sarah joined Edward for his lessons with Miss Lavinia Keppel. Weekends were spent either with the Queen Mother at Royal Lodge or at the large cottage Lord Snowdon had renovated, 'The Old House' at Nymans in Sussex. After attending the London day-school Gibbs with his cousin, David was sent to a preparatory school, Ashdown House, chosen for its nearness to 'The Old House'. He did not shine academically and was sent to a 'crammer', Milbrook House, before going onto a progressive co-educational school, Bedales in Hampshire. Sarah had been to a day-school, Frances Holland, not far from Kensington Palace, before she, too, went to Bedales. Brother and sister arrived together, David thirteen and Sarah eleven.

88. Nanny Sumner collecting David Lindley and Sarah Armstrong-Jones from Gibbs,
their London day school, April 1969.

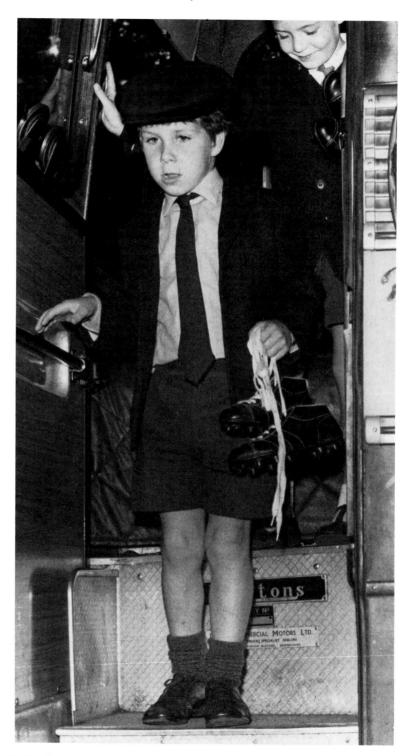

89. David Lindley returning to school from an away football match, October 1968.

90. The Duke and Duchess of Kent with their three children at the Service of Thanksgiving at St Paul's Cathedral to celebrate the Queen's Silver Jubilee, 1977. From the left, the Earl of St Andrews, his sister, Lady Helen Windsor and Lord Nicholas Windsor, yawning. Lord Nicholas Windsor was a page at the wedding of the Prince and Princess of Wales.

When their marriage became severely strained, Princess Margaret and Lord Snowdon decided to send David and Sarah off to the same school at the same time. The formal separation of the parents came a year later in March 1976, and after the automatic divorce, custody of the children was given to Princess Margaret, although David and Sarah are on equally good terms with both parents.

David was better remembered at school for his artistic and woodworking ability rather than for any academic record and he has since gone on to the John Makepeace School for Craftsmen in Dorset where he made his cousin, Charles, his wedding present of a dining-table. Sarah is also heading for an artistic career in taking her 'A' levels in social biology and art and design.

While the diminutive David fights shy of the public eye, Sarah is reasonably well-known, being much in demand as a bridesmaid. Princess Anne chose her for her wedding in 1973 as did Lady Sarah Spencer for her marriage to Neil McCorquodale seven years later. Her greatest role to date, however, was to act as chief bridesmaid at the wedding of the Prince and Princess of Wales.

King George V always thought that Prince George, his fourth son, was the most intelligent of all his children, and that intelligence, as well as his and Princess Marina's fabulous good looks, seem to have come out in the present Duke and Duchess of Kent's children, the Earl of St Andrews, his sister, the Lady Helen Windsor and their younger brother, Lord Nicholas Windsor.

George Philip Nicholas Windsor, the eldest son, was born at Coppins, the Duke and Duchess of Kent's former home in Iver, Buckinghamshire, on 26 June 1962. When only six months old, George spent a year in Hong Kong where his father was serving as a captain in the Royal Scots Greys. His sister, Helen Marina Lucy Windsor, was born just three days before Sarah Armstrong-Jones, on 28 April 1964. Brother and sister grew up together at Coppins and, like their father, uncle and aunt, were treated no differently to any other children in the neighbourhood. Their first great shock came, as we have seen, with the IRA plot to kidnap George from his preparatory school, Heatherdown. The fears proved groundless but it made the Duke and Duchess realise just how vulnerable they and their family were at Coppins. They decided to sell up and move to a house on the Sandringham estate, Anmer Hall, for their country residence, and to York House for their London residence.

At Heatherdown, George was particularly bright and scored a royal first by winning a scholarship to Eton. His sister, Helen, was at school not far away at St Mary's, Wantage in Oxfordshire before moving to Gordonstoun to take her 'A' levels. So far the only public mark that Nicholas, the youngest child, has made is as a page at the wedding of the Prince and Princess of Wales.

The last 'set' of cousins are the children of Princess Alexandra and the Honourable Angus Ogilvy. James Robert Bruce Ogilvy has the rare birthday of 29 February 1964 and his sister, Marina, was born on 31 July 1966. With just ten days between James and Prince Edward, they have been close friends all their lives. James went to Buckingham Palace for his early lessons with Edward and they both went on to the day-preparatory school of Gibbs in Knightsbridge in London. Later he joined his cousin, George St Andrews, at Eton, which he left in the summer of 1981. Marina and James have inherited much of their mother's charm and are recognised as the most amusing and lively of 'the cousins'.

In August 1980, Lady Diana Spencer, aged just nineteen, was asked to stay on board the Royal Yacht *Britannia* for Cowes week, ostensibly to join what was a

91. James and Marina Ogilvy, the children of the Hon. Angus Ogilvy and Princess Alexandra, at the Royal Tournament, Earls Court, London, July 1978.

young party of Andrew, Edward, James and Marina. Today, the Princess of Wales has become the link between this 'younger set' and the older generation of the Royal Family. They are considerably closer to her in age than her husband and his friends. As she herself left school comparatively recently, she shares that same brand of humour, outlook and modern taste as her cousins-in-law. With the exception of Nicholas Windsor, these cousins are now on the brink of adulthood. They, in their turn, will marry and have children, and will, with the children of the Prince and Princess of Wales, provide the next royal generation.

CONCLUSION

Throughout history, royal children have invariably had the most difficult and complex childhoods compared to contemporaries of lesser rank, and it is only with the younger generations of the Royal Family that their upbringing has even approached 'normality'.

In the Middle Ages, the chances of a royal baby surviving through childhood to adulthood were poor. Infant mortality was high, medical knowledge scant, disease rife and political intrigue common. Generally, there were few ties of affection between parents and the medieval royal child. The baby was handed over at birth to a wet-nurse and then to a governor, or lady governor, usually well apart from their parents in their own establishment. The children only became useful to their parents from the age of about ten, when they were considered old enough to fight or to make a politically advantageous marriage. Little changed throughout the Tudor Age except that the children, particularly the girls, were better educated. Stuart children in the seventeenth century fared better than their predecessors, leading a closer family life, while the upbringing of Hanoverian children depended largely on their parents. George I, for instance, took little interest in his grandchildren and even left the eldest, Frederick Louis, in Hanover until he was twenty-one. In turn, Frederick was a good father to his five boys and four girls, but he predeceased his father, George II, after a blow from a cricket ball when playing with his children. His heir, the eldest son who became George III, was initially a devoted father to his fifteen children, but their upbringing, although loving, was spartan and unconventional. For reasons of economy, they spent much of their time isolated in uncomfortable houses grouped round Kew Green on the outskirts of London.

The basic pattern set by Queen Victoria and Prince Albert for their own children, tempered by Victoria's experiences of childhood, has survived up to the latest generation of the Royal Family. The reason for such continuity is that each royal parent over the last 150 years has been faced with the identical problem of trying to raise their children to be normal, unassuming and unaffected while at the same time preparing them for their role in life ahead as useful members of the Royal Family.

(a)

92. The Prince and Princess of Wales's first child will have a number of cousins close in age—and as neighbours, both at Kensington Palace and near Highgrove. They include (a) Peter and Zara Phillips, seen here with Princess Anne after Zara's christening, July 1981 (b) Lord Frederick and Lady Gabriella Windsor, seen here with their parents, after 'Ella's' christening in June 1981, and (c) Lady Rose Windsor, in the arms of her mother, the Duchess of Gloucester, with the five-year-old Earl of Ulster. The Duke of Gloucester is also holding their elder daughter, Lady Davina Windsor with Lady Sarah Armstrong-Jones. Prince Edward helps with the controls. July 1980.

(b)

(c)

The Princess of Wales was born a commoner and her upbringing was typical of any privileged English background. Up to her wedding at the age of twenty, she had led a totally conventional life. She had shown a marked love for children and babies and demonstrated her skill with them by helping out friends and relations with their offspring and at a kindergarten school. She has always been fiercely maternal, with definite ideas about how her own children would be brought up. On the other hand, the Prince of Wales initially had a cloistered royal upbringing before his more liberal parents sent him away to school. Despite the differing backgrounds and childhoods of the Prince and Princess of Wales, the pattern and lifestyle of their first-born baby, William, is, however, largely predictable.

William is a royal child of popular royal parents as well as being second in line to the throne. As such, he will naturally be brought up as royalty and so the Prince and Princess of Wales will have the identical problems as their forebears, although in this modern age of television and extreme popularity of the Royal Family, they will, however, experience even greater problems in that quarter.

Before photographs could be easily reproduced in newspapers, royal children, like the children of King George V, could move about in public with comparative anonymity and freedom. In the next generation, Princess Elizabeth was enormously popular and was instantly recognised on the few occasions she came out in public as a result of the photographs of her that appeared in the press, in books and in other royal ephemera. In turn, there was enormous interest, fuelled by the press, in her son, Prince Charles. Despite the fact that there was virtually no television and only a few newsreels in the cinema when he was very young, he became instantly recognisable. As he grew up, public interest escalated. For example, when he went away to his preparatory school, a newspaper article of one sort or another appeared on sixty-eight out of the eighty-eight days of his first term. Such coverage of royal children could be contained by announcements from Buckingham Palace. Today, however, the public adulation of the Princess of Wales and the insatiable clamour for photographs and reports of William, will inevitably put an added pressure on both parents and child.

By chance, there has always been a nanny or governess still in royal service who could take charge of new royal babies. For a short time, Baroness Lehzen, who cared for Queen Victoria as a child, looked after her two eldes children; the Reverend John Dalton who tutored King George V as a boy was brought back to teach his children, while the faithful 'Alla' Knight was nanny to both the Queen Mother and her daughters. Nanny Lightbody came from the Gloucester brothers when Prince Charles was born, while Mabel Anderson, who was nanny to all the Queen's children, went on to look after Princess Anne's first child, Peter. Breaking with that tradition, the Princess of Wales has engaged Barbara Barnes, a competent nanny whose skill comes from experience rather than any formal training. She is remembered by the Tennant family for her ability to create an ordered and happy nursery where the children were never bored nor idle.

93. The exterior of Apartments 8 and 9, Kensington Palace, the London home of the Prince and Princess of Wales. They finally moved in, after extensive renovations, in May 1982.

Since the reign of Queen Victoria, each successive royal parent has taken particular pleasure in having their children with then whenever possible. Just as George V built on a nursery wing at York Cottage for his expanding family and the Queen Mother made the nurseries for her children at 145 Piccadilly, Buckingham Palace and Royal Lodge, so the Princess of Wales has created her nurseries for William at their two homes, Highgrove in Gloucestershire and their apartments 8 and 9 at Kensington Palace in London. With particular care, she has had them decorated in red, white and blue, choosing the furniture to match.

In very much the same vein as Queen Alexandra when she was Princess of Wales with her five children and the Queen with her two younger sons, the present Princess of Wales will insist, whenever her extensive duties allow, that she cares for her baby herself. It would be very much in character for the Princess to take charge completely of the royal nursery, with the nanny playing a secondary role, a complete departure from traditional royal practice.

Another departure from the traditional royal nursery is one of thrift and economy. In every age, royal children have been brought up frugally, with both food and clothing. George III's children all complained that there was never enough to eat while the nursery staff who cared for Queen Victoria's children, all from working-class families, declared they ate better at home than their royal charges. Food has always been simple in the royal nursery—even the Prince of Wales admits that his favourite nursery fare was boiled chicken and rice and that he found boarding school food too rich. The Princess of Wales, in this case not handicapped with a royal upbringing, will not allow the inherent 'Scots' canny streak' of the Royal Family to enter her nursery, although both parents are careful and practical. As her own taste in clothes has created new fashions, so the baby clothes she chooses for William will instantly be copied. Such a trend follows the sudden rush for yellow baby clothes worn by Princess Elizabeth over fifty years ago. As the first-born, there will be no 'hand-me-downs' common in the Royal Family, like those that went through Queen Victoria's children or from Princess Elizabeth to her younger sister.

Family and close friends are everything to both the Prince and Princess of Wales. Although she comes from what is now termed a 'broken home', the Princess has prized her family above all else, while Prince Charles believes 'that the family unit is the most important aspect of our particular society' which 'insures that the majority of people are subject to an influence and atmosphere of love.' With the birth of William, such a 'unit' has begun in their family. Throughout history, royal children were isolated from their contemporaries, so that they had to rely for friendship on their brothers, sisters or adult members of the Household. Today, such close restrictions are totally out of date. Just as the last set of royal cousins, headed by the Queen's younger sons, are close friends, so William will have a nucleus of friends in his cousins who are close contemporaries. Near to Highgrove are Princess Anne's two children, Peter and Zara Phillips, while close in the opposite direction are Prince and Princess Michael of Kent's two young children, Freddie and Ella. Two of the Duke and

94. The front elevation of Highgrove House, near Tetbury, Gloucestershire, the country home of the Prince and Princess of Wales.

Duchess of Gloucester's three children are rather too old for William, as Alexander is eight and Davina nearly five years his senior, but Rose is only two years older. Although they live in Northamptonshire, the Gloucesters, as well as the Kents, are neighbours in Kensington Palace. Also within the precincts of the Palace are the Princess of Wales's sister, Lady Jane and her husband, Robert Fellowes. Their daughter, Laura, two years William's senior, will undoubtedly become a boon companion in the future. As both the Prince and Princess of Wales know the value of close and trusted friends, neither will allow their children to become as isolated or introverted as were so many of their lonely forebears.

Within the Royal Family, the conflict between the love of their children and a deep sense of duty is far from a novel problem. Long tours of the Empire and Commonwealth separated King George V and Queen Mary from their children for six months at a time. King George VI and Queen Elizabeth, as Duke and Duchess of York, left the very young Princess Elizabeth for six months, just as she had to leave Prince Charles and Princess Anne on her first Commonwealth Tour as Queen in 1953 which also lasted six months. With the resolve and determination of the present Princess of Wales, she will contrive to have William with her as much as possible and that will certainly include the longer royal tours abroad. Despite a heavy schedule, both she and Prince Charles should, with careful planning, be able to be with William for most of the time, for, with a few exceptions, their official duties should emanate from either of their two homes, Highgrove or Kensington Palace.

Where the day-to-day running of the household and general nursery routine is left to the Princess of Wales, the decisions as to the overall planning and education of William, the second in line to the throne, will be ultimately up to Prince Charles. The decision is, however, fairly clear-cut, based on a tried and proved system. Like every other royal child in history, a governess will be appointed to start William off with his lessons with a few other chosen pupils. Then, as it is no longer the exception but the rule that members of the Royal Family want their children to be educated as much like other children as possible, William will be sent away to school.

Above all, the Prince and Princess of Wales will want to carry on that royal anomaly which must be so perplexing to the royal child—never to consider themselves above others, particularly servants, when all the time they are set apart by their birth, the grandeur of their palaces, their relations and the deference shown to them and their family by everyone they meet. For William, this task will be easier than for most of his predecessors, if the press allow, and the reason will lie with his parents. There is no 'school of royalty' where the child learns to be 'royal'. Such skills are acquired by the example of the parents, by watching them and later emulating them. Diana was born a commoner and has ably demonstrated that she has the common touch, being totally at ease with whoever she meets. She is straightforward and practical with good, sound commonsense. The Prince of Wales, on the other hand, upholds the traditions of the Royal Family, while at the same time he has adapted his role as Heir Apparent to the present-day. William will inherit that invaluable mixture of qualities from both parents and it is exactly those qualities that have such tremendous popular appeal today.

SELECTED BIBLIOGRAPHY

Airlie, Mabel, Countess of, *Thatched with Gold* (1962)

Alexandria of Yugoslavia, HM Queen, *Prince Philip, a Family Portrait* (1969)

Ashdown, Dulcie M., *Royal Children* (1979)

Battiscombe, Georgina, *Queen Alexandra* (1969)

Bennett, Daphne, *Queen Victoria's Children* (1980)

Beaton, Cecil, *Royal Portraits* (1963)

Broadley, A., *The Boyhood of a great King* (1906)

Campbell, Judith, *Anne, Portrait of a Princess* (1970)

Cathcart, Helen, *Princess Alexandra* (1969)
 The Duchess of Kent (1971)
 Princess Margaret (1974)

Crawford, Marion, *The Little Princesses* (1950)

Dempster, Nigel, *HRH The Princess Margaret* (1982)

Donaldson, Frances, *Edward VIII* (1974)

Edgar, Donald, *Prince Andrew* (1980)

Fisher, Graham, *Prince Andrew* (1979)

Fisher, Graham & Heather, *Monarchy and the Royal Family* (1979)

Frankland, Noble, *Prince Henry, Duke of Gloucester* (1980)

Gathorne-Hardy, Jonathan, *The Rise and Fall of the British Nanny* (1972)

Gore, John, *King George V, a Personal Memoir* (1941)

Holden, Anthony, *Charles, Prince of Wales* (1979)

Honeycombe, Gordon (with Nicholas Courtney) *Royal Wedding* (1981)

Hudson, Derek, *Kensington Palace* (1968)

Judd, Denis, *Prince Philip, a Biography* (1980)

Lane, Peter, *Prince Philip* (1980)

Lacey, Robert, *Majesty, Elizabeth II and the House of Windsor* (1977)

Liversidge, Douglas, *Prince Charles, Monarch in the Making* (1975)

Magnus, Philip, *King Edward the Seventh* (1964)

Montague-Smith, Patrick & Montgomery-Massingberd, Hugh,
 Royal Palaces, Castles and Homes (1981)

Nicolson, Harold, *King George V, his life and Reign* (1952)

Pope-Hennessy, James, *Queen Mary, 1867–1953* (1959)

Ring, Anne, *The Story of Princess Elizabeth* (1930)

Plowden, Alison, *The Young Victoria* (1981)

St Aubyn, the Hon. Giles, *Edward VII, Prince and King* (1979)
    William of Gloucester, Pioneer Prince (1977)

Sinclair, David, *Queen and Country, the Life of Queen Elizabeth the Queen Mother* (1979)

Wheeler-Bennett, Sir John *King George VI, His life and Reign* (1958)

Windsor, HRH the Duke of, *A King's Story* (1951)
    A Family Album (1960)

Woodham-Smith, Cecil, *Queen Victoria, her Life and Times* (1972)

York, Rosemary, *Charles In His Own Words* (1981)

INDEX